COLLE

Handbook for Assessing and Managing Care in the Community

of related interest

Caring for People in the Community
The New Welfare
Edited by Mike Titterton
ISBN 1 85302 112 1

Handbook of Theory for Practice Teachers in Social Work
Edited by Joyce Lishman
ISBN 1 85302 098 2

Introducing Network Analysis in Social Work
Philip Seed
ISBN 1 85302 034 6 hb
ISBN 1 85302 106 7 pb

Performance Review and Quality Assurance in Social Work
Edited by Anne Connor and Stewart Black
ISBN 1 85302 017 6
Research Highlights in Social Work 20

Handbook for Assessing and Managing Care in the Community

Philip Seed and Gillian Kaye

Jessica Kingsley Publishers
London and Bristol, Pennsylvania

First published in the United Kingdom in 1994 by
Jessica Kingsley Publishers Ltd
116 Pentonville Road
London N1 9JB, England
and
1900 Frost Road, Suite 101
Bristol, PA 19007, U S A

Copyright © 1994 Philip Seed and Gillian Kaye

Library of Congress Cataloging in Publication Data
Seed, Philip.
Handbook for Assessing and Managing Care in the Community /
Philip Seed and Gillian Kaye
p. cm.
Includes bibliographical references and index.
ISBN 1-85302-227-6 (pbk.)
1. Handicapped--Care. 2. Handicapped--Care__Scotland. I. Kaye,
Gillian, 1953- . II. Title
HV1568.S39 1994
362.4'0485'09411--dc20

British Library Cataloguing in Publication Data
Seed, Philip
Handbook for Assessing and Managing
Care in the Community
I. Title II. Kaye, Gillian
362.40485

ISBN 1-85302-227-6

Printed and Bound in Great Britain by
Biddles Ltd., Guildford and King's Lynn

Contents

List of Figures

Introduction

This book aims to fill two main gaps in assisting social services staff and others concerned with assessment and care management.

First, it gets beyond general guidelines to day-to-day practical issues facing those carrying out assessments. It looks at both the skills and the knowledge required by staff to undertake assessments and helps staff to understand the broader meaning and context of specific assessment tasks they may be asked to undertake.

Second, the book concentrates on making the necessary, but often lacking, links between assessment techniques and procedures and care management. Care management involves resource allocation and planning. The problem of linkage is approached from each direction, namely:

1. What kind of assessment will provide the information for effective resource allocation and planning?

2. What kind of resource allocation procedures will ensure the closest links with individual client assessments?

We do not claim to cover other aspects of care in the community (for example screening procedures, inspection, etc).

The book is informed by recent research including major research carried out by the authors and colleagues, funded by the Scottish Office (Social Work Services Group), into Assessment, Resource Allocation and Planning for Adults with Learning Difficulties in Supported Accommodation in Scotland. While drawing on this research experience, as well as other smaller and related research undertaken by Dr Seed and others, implications are drawn from the authors' broader experience for working with other client groups, especially elderly people and people with physical as well as multiple disabilities, people with mental health problems and people with HIV and AIDS. Another application of particular concern to the authors is for work with young people leaving residential social services establishments or special schools.

The assessment processes which were studied focused mainly on people in residential and supported accommodation settings in the community and those preparing to move to such settings. The moves comprised:

1. People moving from hospitals to staffed residential settings in the community.

2. People moving on from staffed residential settings in the community to more independent forms of supported accommodation, such as supported tenancies.

3. People leaving the care of relatives for either staffed or un-staffed supported accommodation.

4. People living on their own requiring staffed residential accommodation.

The first chapter, 'Developing Excellence in Community Care', explores the difficulties of maintaining the ideals of care in the community – namely, a needs-led person-centred approach – in the face of resource and procedural constraints. What do the ideals mean in identifying and carrying out everyday care tasks effectively? The first stage in answering this question is to establish what good standards are – a question of moving beyond statements of principles to the implications for daily practice. These statements of good practice are based on empirical research findings.

Chapters Two to Four examine different aspects of the assessment process. First, traditional assessment approaches are considered and largely rejected because they tried to slot people into categories of dependency rather than to look at opportunities for developing individual assets. An approach is recommended which emphasises support to enhance opportunities in order to improve quality of life. These terms are discussed and applied to the question of client choice (Chapter Three) and the skills needed to carry out assessments (Chapter Four).

Chapter Five addresses the issue of how best to move on from an individual client assessment of needs to the notion of placement 'packages' – in other words, to a coherent care plan. It spotlights the likely areas of difficulty and suggests ways of overcoming them.

Chapter Six looks at techniques for costing services and carefully examines issues arising from a traditional 'unit' costs approach. An alternative 'real costs' procedure is recommended and explained. This is then used to illuminate some important service costing issues, including cost-effectiveness, for people with higher support needs in staffed accommodation, compared with those with lower support needs in un-staffed units. Another issue discussed is the care management situation in a residential setting when some clients move out, leaving others behind.

These considerations lead on to looking at an overall approach to resource allocation and placement planning. Informed by the research in areas within five Scottish Regions, a number of major conclusions are drawn for the best planning approach along a continuum from centralisation to what we call 'localisation'.

In the final chapter, care management issues are summarised in the case of people who we can say have 'very special needs', including adults with profound intellectual and physical disabilities, and people with multiple disabilities, potentially life-threatening illnesses or challenging behaviour and people with serious addictions.

This book is written in the wake of a myriad of official statements in various forms explaining or offering guidelines for care in the community. We do not intend to refer extensively to these or even to attempt to summarise them; but the dust has settled sufficiently for us to attempt to discern directions in terms of philosophy and policies which have implications for tasks and skills to promote 'excellence' in practice.

The book is addressed to care managers and to social care providers, including staff at all levels. We hope it will also be helpful to other staff in the health and social services who are concerned with the implementation of care in the community.

ACKNOWLEDGEMENTS

Gratitude is expressed to all our past and present colleagues at the University of Dundee. Their advice continues to be invaluable.

Gratitude must also be expressed to the various bodies who have funded research and consultancy work which has helped to inform this book, both in terms of the development of the assessment approach described in Chapter Two and in terms of the many examples given. (The actual examples are, of course, fictitious or based on examples which have been disguised.)

Particular thanks to:

- The Scottish Office, Social Work Services Group, who have been sponsoring major and minor research projects undertaken by Philip Seed and colleagues, first at Aberdeen and latterly at Dundee Universities for the past 20 years. Gill Kaye was one of the team in the most recent research into Assessment, Resource Allocation and Planning, completed last year. Work has also been commissioned by the Scottish Education Department into social aspects of integration in schools.

- Cornerstone Community Care (Aberdeen) who have also been commissioning work for many years, including recent work.

- The Economic and Social Research Council

- The Mental Health Foundation

- Local Authorities, especially Highland and Grampian Regions' Social Work Departments and, recently Mid-Kent SSD.

- Many voluntary bodies, including the White Top Foundation, the Scott Foundation, AVEYRON Parents' Group (Hamilton and East Kilbride), Quarriers, Raddery School.

This book could not have been written without the first-hand experience gained in this work.

Finally, we must stress that the views expressed in this book are the views of the authors and that the various research and training bodies whose support is acknowledged are in no way committed to these views.

CHAPTER ONE

Developing Excellence in Community Care

'Care in the community' or 'community care' has come to represent both a philosophy and a policy in the United Kingdom with respect to the provision of personal social services for adults. It is important to distinguish between the two.

The philosophy of care in the community includes the following four elements:

1. *'Quality of life'*. Quality of life criteria should be adopted for assessing people's needs for support in personal care and daily living in the community. 'Quality of life' includes material, social and spiritual wellbeing in a safe environment.

2. *Individualisation*. An integrated and individualised response to assessed needs on the part of the health and social services.

3. *Participation*. A participatory approach to the provision of services, emphasising personal choice.

4. *Developing potential*. Building on existing or potential sources of support from relatives, friends, neighbourhood resources and other components of people's social networks.

These philosophical principles or precepts should not be confused with the following aspects of current social policy:

1. The closing down of some long-stay hospitals, and reduction in size of others, leading to the rehabilitation of patients 'in the community'.

2. A re-definition of the role of local authority services from main provider of facilities to enabler or facilitator.

3. Assessments being framed in terms of client needs instead of in terms of the parameters of services available from a given source.

4. The quest for 'value for money' in the provision of appropriate services pursued by various means including

    (i) separation between service purchasers and providers

    (ii) monitoring and inspection of services.

There are both links and tensions between the philosophy and the policy of community care.

They are linked by the idea of a market economy in health and social welfare. The market economy is promoted both as a means and as an end. It is claimed to be a means to the more effective delivery of health and social services. It is also claimed to be the best approach to an economic, social and political order more generally, which will provide for a higher shared quality of life.

At the same time, the operation of the market imposes severe constraints on state provision. Here, then, is a source of tension between the philosophy of community care and the policies associated with it.

'Market welfare' has partly replaced 'state welfare'. But we still have care in the community as an expression of social policy in recognition of what we may call a continuing (and in some respects even a growing) sense of shared societal responsibility. The tension between hard-nosed economics or finance, and altruism with regard to living with one another as a community, is very great. This is the context for understanding what care in the community means and how social workers, health care staff and others perceive, and try to carry out, new tasks.

It also provides the context for defining 'excellence' in community care. For those who like diagrams, we have tried to represent some of these complex themes in Figure 1a.

A distinction can be made between the national policy of care in the community and different local authority interpretations of that policy, especially concerning the role of the care manager. The issues at a more local level are summarised in Figure 1b.[*] This

---

[*]   Based on material from the University of Dundee's distance learning pack *Planning and Managing Community Care*.

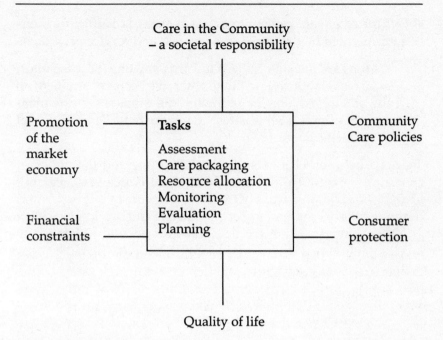

Figure 1a Care in the Community

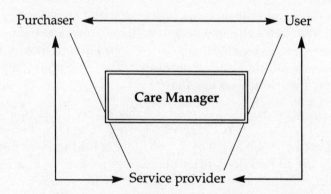

*Re-drawn with kind permission from Denis Rowley, University of Dundee Social Work Department.

*Figure 1b 'The Care Manager's Web'**

shows the care management role drawn towards conflicting interests represented by the purchaser, the user and service providers:

> As the care manager moves towards any one (of these interests) the relationship with the other two becomes strained; on the other hand, staying in the middle exposes the care manager to a high level of stress. (University of Dundee, Social Work Department 1993)

Tensions between elements of the philosophy and the policy of community care arise not only because of scarce resources but because of traditional ways of thinking. The core of this problem is the conventional separation between needs and services.

Needs have traditionally been categorised with reference to labelling individual clients – for example, people who have:

- learning disabilities
- mental health problems
- dementia
- AIDS
- physical disabilities

In other words, we have asked, for example, 'What are the special needs of people with learning disabilities?'

This way of thinking produces tension with the philosophy of community care because, first, some individuals fall into different categories (for example an elderly person with Down's syndrome suffering from dementia, or a person with both physical and mental disabilities). Second, individuals, in any case, do not live in isolation from one another and community care is all about support *between* people. Here is an example:

> Mr A, aged 37, used to attend a day centre for people with learning disabilities. He saw no point in attending because it did not help him to get a job and more of his time was needed at home to help look after his elderly mother with a severe heart condition following a stroke. A nurse attends daily. There are no other family members nearby, although Mr A's younger brother visits about once a month from a city 40 miles away. The brother's wife is disabled and he cannot on this account spend more time with his mother.

This short statement invokes the possibility of categories of different services, viewed on traditional lines:

- Day services for people with learning disabilities
- Employment services
- Supported accommodation away from home for people with learning disabilities
- Residential accommodation for elderly people or people with physical disabilities
- Domiciliary support services
- Respite services (themselves categorised)

But the family do not want or need categories of services: they need a single, coherent response to their family situation. Such a response, in accordance with the philosophy of community care, will emphasise choice. For example:

- How, and to what extent, does Mr A want to be involved in helping to care for his mother?
- How, and to what extent, does the mother want to be cared for by family members?

In the light of these wishes, we may determine whether mother and son will remain and be supported as a living unit, or whether, for example:

Mr A leaves home (still, perhaps, able to offer some support). Mother goes into residential or other supported accommodation (remaining, perhaps, in contact with her sons).

The above would represent a way of looking at the family situation from the point of view of a needs-led assessment and care management. To be effective, the services and the professional disciplines have to be geared to thinking in these terms, free of the conceptual limitations we have outlined.

Care management, then, involves the interplay of:

- Resources – and decisions regarding their allocation and targeting.
- The way services are perceived and organised.
- Professional knowledge and skills at all levels of the process.

The last mentioned core factor on which the others depend.

Professional knowledge and skills fall into several categories:

1. Knowledge base

Those responsible for assessment and care management should have the experience and training to make responsible and informed judgements about needs. If care management is to be individualised this must be able to be made specific to individual circumstances. In other words, if the client has dementia or, for example, a rare syndrome, those involved must know, or be able to find out, about these conditions and their social implications. Second, there should be exhaustive knowledge available about local community resources. Third, a knowledge of rights, entitlements, procedures and the legal position of the client is essential.

2. Negotiating skills

Negotiation takes place at the interface between competing interests. In this case, the interface is principally between applying excellence in terms of the philosophy of community care and the other interests of community care policy, which we have outlined.

In the care management process, different staff will represent different sets of interests. We say 'sets of interests' rather than simply 'interests' because within each set there will also often be competing interests. For example, in the case of the A Family whose situation we summarised earlier, the interests of Mr A may compete with his mother's interests. There are also competing sets of interests within the health and social services: interests of purchasers and providers, financial and service managers, managers and policy-makers.

In this respect traditional models of accountability in terms of 'line management' are not sufficient for care in the community. The scenario of accountability must now take into account inspection units, consumer rights, consumer groups, as well as line management.

3. Assessment skills

These include understanding different kinds of assessment, participating with the client and knowing how to make the information usefully available to others. Assessment skills appear to be a neglected aspect of community care thus far and form the main topic of Chapter Four.

4. Direct care skills

The manager must be aware of what direct care skills entail. These form the bedrock on which any successful community care must rest. The nature of the requirements will vary from the very personal, intimate physical assistance and loving concern of a carer sharing their home, to whatever professional functions are involved in enabling people to carry out the things they want to do, or do better, for themselves. 'Support' may be a more helpful term than 'care' here, as the context for any necessary physical care is personal support.

AN UNDERSTANDING OF CLIENT NEEDS

The care manager has to make judgements about client needs. Statements about 'needs' seldom have an empirical base. To provide such a base, we will examine support needs in some detail in the light of a study by the authors of the needs of, and services received by, 41 clients in representative forms of supported accommodation in the period leading up to April 1993.

It could be relatively straightforward to determine the sorts of support a given client needs using traditional categories, such as health problems – mobility – literacy – day care – and so forth. However, good practice in community care requires a broad vision of the possibilities of securing the best quality of life for the client and the willingness to look for and even create opportunities to improve it.

The study referred to elicited information both about the support services already received and the support which would be required, either to improve the quality of life or under changed living circumstances (for example if given greater independence). By drawing together the best parts of the collective results, an impression can be created of the elements which constitute an effective, good quality support service.

The most basic human needs become an issue when the focus is on people who have difficulty procuring such necessities for themselves. The complexity of the arrangements for obtaining, for example, housing, or an income sufficient to support even a limited quality of life, is very great.

An integrated approach to meeting a person's support needs therefore requires first a check to see whether the best forms of support and service are being received at the level of basic human needs. Assuming these are in place on a physical level, there are also basic psychological needs which require to be addressed.

BASIC HUMAN NEEDS – PHYSICAL

1. A bed and a room

A single room was preferred by all respondents in the study. (It has been put to us that in a Camphill Community room-sharing may be an accepted part of communal life.) The desire to share with a friend was not mentioned in our study by anyone living alone. The bedroom should be a place where a person feels safe. Other residents who are prone to be noisy or violent can be a serious source of anxiety. One feature of institutional living can be that the decor and furnishings are standard issue or inherited from a previous occupant, whereas to choose these things for oneself can add enormously to a sense of wellbeing and belonging and being in some control.

> *Good practice favours allowing clients the right to a single room where they feel safe, and where they can choose their own decor and furnishings.*

2. Food

Ideally, clients should be able to choose their meals and, as far as they are able and it is safe, cook for themselves. Some living in group situations had no choice or kitchen opportunities, while others were able to buy and cook their own food, or at least have a say in the meal planning. The constraints on this were sometimes due to budgeting arrangements and the employed cook's contract, sometimes lack of kitchen facilities (hardly a sufficient explanation for a client being denied the opportunity to make coffee or toast), and sometimes lack of staff time to supervise kitchen activities. It would appear that this is an area where resources, both in the form of safe, user-friendly kitchen equipment and personnel – perhaps volunteers or family members – could enhance the quality of life at small cost.

On the other hand, an important support skill is to help the client who does have responsibility for her or his own meals to choose a healthy, balanced diet, especially as the ever-present opportunity to spend small amounts of money on snacks and drinks can make the preparation of a proper meal seem like too much hard work.

> *Good practice means clients having control over what food they eat and how it is prepared, and having the opportunity to prepare food themselves if they are able to, with the support and advice they need to benefit from a healthy diet.*

3. Clothing

Clients may be expected to have clear views about the styles they wish to wear. However, the adults with learning disabilities in the study appeared to have few opportunities to shop alone or to spend money in the amounts required for clothing. Those clients who were unable to check change or handle more than small amounts of money could only buy clothes for themselves with supervision. The demands placed on staff by this appeared to have led in many cases to staff purchasing clothes on behalf of clients, with the attendant problems of size/fit and suitability. The ideal would be for all clients to receive the same attention to enhancing their looks as that received by those being cared for at home, where garments are altered to ensure perfect fit, and a personal pride is taken by the carer in the loved one's appearance.

> *Good practice means promoting comfort and a sense of personal worth through choosing clothes and what to wear. It means giving appropriate support to clients to buy their own clothes and the opportunity to personalise them (for example by altering them).*

4. Shelter and Heating

Such everyday events as controlling the environmental tempera-ture can be a problem for the person with learning disabilities. This is not apparent when there are other people around to control the heating and open and close the windows as necessary, but advice and guidance will be required by those living independently, particularly in order to keep fuel bills manageable.

> *Good practice will ensure that clients have practical help to enable them to control their daily living environment.*

5. Safety and wellbeing

The greatest anxiety of parents of children with learning disabilities is 'Who will look after our son or daughter when we are not able?' This highlights a dependency which, unlike most childhood dependencies, those affected do not grow out of. The situation of many forms of care in the community puts upon the carer a responsibility for the wellbeing and safety of adults who in some cases do not accept or understand their own need for supervision. Where the parameters of safety and good practice in the supervision of children are fairly well defined, the issue of what is acceptable in terms of personal freedom for the adult recipient of care and what constitutes acceptable risk to his own safety are much less well defined.

Thus a carer making day-to-day decisions about whether a client can be left alone in the kitchen making tea, or whether another will manage to cross the road safely while walking to the local shop, is taking responsibility for potentially life-threatening situations. The balance between infringing an adult's rights and protecting him is a difficult one. Some clients have unrealistic expectations of how well they will be able to manage their lives in the community, for example in cooking for themselves, and become upset when they discover how difficult they find it. It is equally the case that professionals and parents may have expectations of clients which are too low, and not allow them to reach their potential. The staff comment on one woman who moved out of a hostel into a flat was: 'A different person since she left. She surprised us all'.

If some emergency, such as illness, fire, or so forth happens during the night, most people would require help, but gaining that help can be more problematic for a client living alone or in unstaffed group living situations. For example, many clients are unsure about how to use the telephone, which would commonly be the first means of calling for help. In fact, a telephone is not always supplied for clients who have difficulty speaking to people

they do not know well, or difficulty making themselves understood, especially when excited. These difficulties could also cause
problems in alerting the neighbours who would be the other main
source of help 'out of hours'. In situations where supervision is not
on the spot, it is vital that the client has ready access to help during
the night.

Much of the above applies also to elderly clients suffering from
dementia, only in this case the carer is more likely to be a daughter,
sister or son.

> *Good practice will ensure maximum safety in all its aspects*
> *consistent with allowing acceptable risk-taking in developing*
> *opportunities in daily living.*

6. Access to medical attention, dentist, chiropodist, hairdresser

Clients can be unable or unwilling to make their needs known in
order to have an appointment made, and access to such services
needs to be made as easy as possible to prevent serious omissions.

> *Good practice ensures client's rights to the best available dental,*
> *chiropody, and hairdressing services in accordance with their*
> *wishes.*

BASIC PSYCHOLOGICAL NEEDS

1. Security regarding their home

Anxiety was expressed by many clients in the study, most commonly in regard to future living situation, and handling strangers.
Yet it is in the nature of an evolving and developing policy of
community care that changes occur in the accommodation offered
and the living situation of individuals – albeit changes intended to
be for the better in the long run. However, the nature of the
negotiations between agencies and between financial controllers
means that decisions can be delayed, reversed, announced and
then retracted. For those on the receiving end of the provision this
can mean the antithesis of a good quality service when the uncer-
tainty is over the future of vulnerable people who have little control

over their own lives. The task for staff of assuring the residents of continuing care leaves them with the dilemma of either trying to keep them in the dark about the administrative goings-on which will inevitably affect their futures, or expending considerable time and effort to explain to them a situation which most people would despair of describing positively. Such decisions and skills are liable to be extensively in demand in the current climate of changes in administrative responsibility. (These points are discussed further in Chapter Five.)

Many recipients of community care are obliged to accept help in daily living from others whom they did not choose. Given that some clients experience anxiety in meeting new people, changes in support staff are bound to be distressing, the more so if changes occur frequently. While professionals cannot be prevented from moving on to other employment, there may be ways of improving job satisfaction (for example salaries, training, access to policy decisions affecting the clients they work with) which would encourage staff to remain in post and so allow residents to have a greater sense of security about the continuity of their carers.

> Good practice means that clients will feel secure about changes in their home and future moves and that they will be helped to get used to new surroundings.

2. Significant personal relationships

It is usually accepted that family have the right, if not the duty, to visit, take an interest in, and in some cases care for their relatives who are being cared for in the community. In this way family relationships are likely to be sustained or to fade according to the motivation and ability of the family to keep up contact. However, by no means all clients have family, and those who do are unlikely to find all their needs for personal relationships fulfilled through their relatives.

For a considerable number of clients in the study, other people seemingly had a merely functional importance, and many were apparently satisfied with what must have been fairly distant relationships (for example, one named as her 'three best friends' three members of staff at her day centre). It may not be easy for people with difficulties in communication to establish relationships, and there is a real danger of isolation if a resident is moved from a care situation where constant company is almost unavoidable to more independent living.

The opportunity to develop and enjoy friendships depends partly on practicalities such as the location of their home, ability to use public transport, degree of physical handicap, ability to use the phone, financial situation, and so forth. The point of importance for service provision is that it is rather easy to prevent or kill off a precariously developing relationship when one or both parties are adults with learning disabilities or other disabilities. People receiving care often have little opportunity to choose the peers they live with. If they do make a fulfilling friendship they also have little control over how that relationship will be affected by future placement and service decisions. It is therefore necessary that the professionals afford clients' friendships importance in these decisions.

> *Good practice ensures that clients are able to maintain contacts with their relatives and close friends, as well as having opportunities to make new friends.*

3. Privacy

The need for privacy was given by clients in the study as a reason for preferring a single room, and it was given by relatives and staff as a reason for advocating a move out of a hostel to more individual accommodation. Many residents of hostels considered the number they lived with to be too many. (This varied between 3 and 40.) The desire to be alone and be amongst other people only when one chooses is another freedom which is often denied those requiring care. Whilst this is sometimes unavoidable, due to the level of support required, it is a feature of good quality service that it intrudes on the client's personal space to the minimum degree necessary.

> *Good practice ensures clients the right to privacy.*

NEEDS AS MEMBERS OF SOCIETY

There are innumerable other, mainly less vital areas of life, which will be mentioned briefly here, as a pointer to features of good quality care.

1. Access to money

It is an important aspect of encouraging self-confidence and self-respect for people to be able to collect their own allowance at a bank or Post Office within reach, if they are not in the position of earning a wage. This may mean having an escort or transport arranged rather than collecting the money on behalf of the client.

> *Good practice allows people to handle their own money, with appropriate level of guidance.*

2. The opportunity to socialise in the daytime and in the evening

Clients not living in group situations are in danger of being isolated because of lack of confidence to socialise, combined with circumstances which have left them inaccessible to relatives. Other clients have the opposite problem of being inappropriately trusting, and ready to chat to whoever they meet, leading to fears for their safety if allowed to go out and socialise indiscriminately. Beside their many other services, the principal function of the Day Centre or workplace for many clients is a social one.

It was clear from the study that a great variety of evening social events are enjoyed by some clients. The determining factors as to whether a particular client had access to them had little to do with the clients themselves, but seemed to depend on the motivation and availability of escorts, the enthusiasm or otherwise of the local community to run clubs, and the geographical location and availability of suitable transport.

> *Good practice affords clients opportunities to choose to socialise in a variety of ways during the day and in the evening.*

3. Day time occupation

Attendance at a Day Centre or work placement is very important in giving structure to daily life. The choice of some clients in the study to work in the kitchen at their Day Centre, rather than participate in the programmes of activities designed to address their particular needs, illustrates a principle in the provision of care: that a sense of making a worthwhile contribution – 'paying one's way' – is more valued than the receipt of services, however well-planned and interesting.

In the matter of work placements, as in other areas, clients' success in securing some kind of job was related either to skills or to motivation on the part of support workers or to the geographical location, rather than to any attributes of the clients. Given the low expectations in terms of conditions and salaries, a more imaginative approach to finding work placements with good supervision could produce fruit in terms of satisfaction for clients and valuable work being performed.

> *Clients are entitled to support in pursuing equal opportunities in employment. In the absence of employment, or further education, day services provide a necessary structure to daily living, provided it is what clients want to do and provided it is based on their own contribution and not on being merely the recipients of a service.*

4. Shopping

This is a part of everyday life which a good quality service would make available to those whose disabilities would otherwise prevent it, by providing transport, escort, and so forth, as necessary.

> *Good practice enables clients to shop for themselves with necessary support.*

5. Pastimes, sports and hobbies

The application of support workers combined with motivation on the clients' part can lead to a broad range of leisure activities. A few examples will illustrate the range:

- Electric organ, with or without lessons from a music therapist
- CB Radio equipment, and membership of a CB club
- Guide Dogs for the Blind: family involvement with the organisation, in addition to being the owner of a guide dog
- Cycling club – participation in group cycle runs
- Leisure Centres – not only to swim, play bowls, and so forth, but also for those unwilling or unable to participate simply to watch and have a drink
- Church – for both social and spiritual benefits.

> *Good practice recognises the importance of personal interests and hobbies and facilitates opportunities for these to be pursued.*

6. Holidays

The opportunity of a holiday for those who are unable to arrange a break for themselves can be a very great gift indeed, to give workers and clients a break, to widen clients' horizons, and to facilitate socialising. The factors which limit the ability to offer clients holidays are usually finance, and availability of staff. Some clients are able to receive holidays thanks to local charitable funds or organisations. Volunteers can also make the supervision more manageable. The benefits gained from a holiday appear to justify a good deal of effort on the part of the support worker to secure it.

> *Good practice recognises client's entitlement to holidays and the particular opportunities holidays afford.*

7. Further education

The availability of college courses varies from area to area. However, the energies expended by support workers in discovering what is available in the locality and amongst the local groups of enthusiasts can make a world of difference to the life-enhancing opportunities open to clients.

> *Good practice acknowledges clients' rights to further education and facilitates access to courses.*

PROFESSIONAL SKILLS

The support required by individual clients determines the nature of the support tasks, which are themselves inseparable from the skills necessary to achieve them. The following general points can be drawn out of the specific skills involved.

1. Commitment to providing for the client's needs as fully as possible. This means attempting to realise the client's potential to lead a fulfilling life by providing opportunities to learn and develop skills. For many clients this is principally about progress towards independence. In this situation, it is important that staff do, in fact, help the client towards independence and do not contribute to his or her dependency in the support they offer. A further element in encouraging the client's progress towards independence is the commitment to assessment – or at least taking stock – of the progress actually made and adjustments of goals and levels of support in line with changing needs. The primary commitment to attending to client needs also implies respect for all clients (including those less easy to care for) as people with the same rights to self-determination (as far as practicable) as other adults and, accordingly, the importance of treating their views and wishes seriously.

2. Understanding, empathy, compassion, patience and the ability to be positive in handling clients' difficulties in learning or coping.

3. Sensitivity to clients' strengths and weaknesses and the ability to make sound judgements, balancing the relative risks and benefits, in determining the appropriate level of supervision and responsibility afforded to individual clients.

4. Clear judgement as to the ability of a client to seek help successfully and appropriately in unforeseen circumstances, and setting up workable helplines for such eventualities.

5. Application and energy in seeking interesting work placements for clients. Some support staff will have a network of relationships within the locality with people who manage work situations where sheltered placements could be set up; others would be starting from scratch. Skills in negotiation, outlining the client's needs and strengths in a realistic, sympathetic way, and the ability to predict with realism and a fair degree of accuracy what the client's skills and reactions would be, are necessary skills to achieve this task successfully.

6. The ability to accompany and supervise clients in public situations without embarrassment or humiliation for the client, and sensitivity to enable the client to make appropriate purchases when shopping.

7. The motivation and ability to discover new areas of interests, pastimes, sport, holiday, and further education opportunities for clients. This skill involves a belief that new opportunities can be opened up, and a determination to 'make it happen'. The practicalities, as well as good communication skills, involve the ability to make any special arrangements necessary to enable clients to participate. Seeking special treatment for client groups has to be handled sensitively, as to draw attention by requiring special or 'charitable' treatment can work against enabling clients to participate normally in normal activities.

8. In the case of some clients, the necessary skills are related to coping with physical disabilities. These include nursing-type tasks – to do with medication, toileting, and so forth; physical help with such areas as dressing, mobility, and bathing, and in general a patient acceptance of the client's desire to do tasks for himself or herself, however slowly.

9. For clients who require reminding and guidance rather than physical help to cope with self-care tasks such as washing and dressing, what is of vital importance in good quality care is that the help is given with courtesy and respect for the client.

10. Much of the support required by clients, especially adults with learning disabilities, is teaching and support to learn skills, such as cooking, literacy, and use of money. Time and again, support workers in the study expressed disappointment at how little help they were able to offer clients, due to lack of time. Clearly, there are advantages in learning in one's own home, from a known person, in terms of minimising communication difficulties, the lesson content being at an appropriate level, familiarity of teacher and learner with the surroundings, and opportunities to practise outside the lesson time. There is a considerable degree of skill required to teach well, and an extremely valuable investment would be to provide training for care and support workers and also volunteers in the teaching of basic daily living skills.

In conclusion, three main strands run through the discussion of support tasks:

- Provision of adequate care to meet the basic needs of the clients, where they are unable to undertake to do so for themselves

- Offer of opportunities to participate in life-enhancing activities, pursuits and occupations, in a way that recognises clients as having every right to an enjoyable and fulfilling lifestyle

- Enabling and teaching of the skills which lead to greater independence and the ability to meet the world on more equal terms for as long as the client wishes to continue learning.

The support required demands team effort on the part of care and support staff, care managers and higher agency management.

CHAPTER TWO

Quality of Life Assessment

The word 'assessment' has changed its meaning in social work. In the 1950s, when 'casework' followed a medical model, part of what we now call 'assessment' was called 'social diagnosis'. This meant understanding the problems a client presented. Diagnosis was followed by 'assessment', which then meant weighing up the strengths and weaknesses in the situation. This, in turn, was followed by a 'treatment plan'.

'Assessment' in this sense was displaced when a systems approach to planning social work intervention tended to take over from a medical model in the early 1970s. The word 'assessment' does not appear in the index, for example, of Howard Goldstein's *Social Work Practice – a Unitary Approach* (1971). The nearest we come to it is in terms of what is called the 'induction' phase of practice – 'induction' meaning the process of becoming aware of the problems within the various client, change and 'target' systems. The consequence of a systems approach for a later understanding of assessment is perhaps that it helped to broaden the focus of intervention from the 'diagnosis' of the client's immediate family situation to a broader understanding of issues associated with the client and the agency in society.

Derivations from other fields have, perhaps, had a more direct influence on the present meaning of assessment in community care. First, in education and educational psychology 'assessment' has long been associated with attainment and adaptation. Second, in ordinary usage, 'assessment' tended to have financial connotations, as, for example, with a tax assessment.

Elements of these various meanings of assessment were reflected in the traditional assessments that were carried out until recently by local authorities for residential accommodation – for what used to be called 'Part III' accommodation (Part III of the National Assistance Act, 1948). Applicants were assessed financially to see whether they should contribute to the cost, and for eligibility for a place depending partly on their social situation (whether anyone else could look after them) and partly on whether they fitted into the category of service provided. If their support needs were too great, they were rejected because they were judged to be the responsibility of the health authorities. If, on the other hand, they were not great enough, it was considered that domiciliary services would be more appropriate.

Applications for Part III accommodation are an example of a 'service-led' assessment. Clients were assessed for services. The main question the local authority concerned itself with in planning services was 'how many?' How many places in homes were needed, and could be afforded, to fulfil responsibilities under particular legislation?

The situation in Scotland was slightly different from that in England and Wales in this respect. Section 12 of the Social Work (Scotland) Act (1968) gave local authorities the open-ended duty 'to promote social welfare'. This could be interpreted as implying a needs-led approach to planning services in the community.

Meanwhile, the idea of an overall assessment, with more open-ended options for possible services the client might need, slowly developed in other fields: delinquency services, child guidance, psychiatric services and in determining special educational needs following the recognition (with the Warnock Committee Report of 1978) that no child was to be regarded as ineducable. Special educational needs assessments, called 'Statements of Need' (England and Wales) or 'Record of Needs' (Scotland) and Future Needs Assessments of children preparing to leave school, were intended to re-phrase the assessment question from 'Does the child fit into this or that category of need for this or that service?' to 'What service does this child need?'

The idea of a needs-led assessment, then, was not invented with the National Health Service and Community Care Act, 1990. But it was, in many ways, consolidated and the rhetoric gained a new prominence.

One of the main consolidating mechanisms contained within community care policy is the separation of the 'purchaser' of services (i.e., the local authority acting for the client) and the 'provider' of the services required, for example a voluntary or commercial agency or the local authority itself. This, again, is not a new idea. In the field of special education, a local authority has long been the 'purchaser' of special school places.

Experience in the educational field may lead us to question to what extent assessments are 'needs-led' rather than 'service-led'. The question depends on the extent of choice, or 'options'. Recent research into placement outcomes following future needs assessments for young people with multiple disabilities is discouraging in this respect. In many of the cases studied, the people concerned and their parents were only offered one placement choice when the child left a residential special school – 'take it or leave it'. Some parents declined the offer and the young person remained at home, perhaps on a long-term waiting list for something better (Hubbard 1992).

For an assessment to be needs-led rather than service-led there must be a range of options. This is one of the basic principles of assessment in community care.

The quality of the assessment and care management processes as a whole depends on the extent to which assessment enhances the opportunity for individualised and flexible planning of services. No matter how elaborate an assessment might be, the exercise is of no direct value if only one way forward is open.

Two contrasting case examples will illustrate this point.

> George had multiple physical disabilities and a mild learning disability. He was completing a course at a rehabilitation centre. While there he had made many friends, had part-time employment prospects, and wanted to live in the area. However, no housing was available with suitable support. It transpired that it was not the policy of the authorities in the area to encourage people to remain in the locality after their period at the rehabilitation centre (which had a much wider catchment area) had come to an end. George's mother lived in a city over a hundred miles away and George was offered housing in a special project in that city. No other option was seriously considered with him.

By no stretch of the imagination could the process of assessment of George's situation be considered to be 'needs-led' or consistent with the principles of good practice outlined in the last chapter. The only issue the assessment was concerned with was whether or not he would fit into the special housing project in a locality not of his choosing.

Gladys, on the other hand, had a very different experience.

> Gladys was fed up with living with a lot of other people in a staffed hostel for people with learning disabilities. Her wishes and needs were carefully studied and discussed without any preconceptions about where she could, or should, move to. Her assessment took the form of various discussions with different people offering different perspectives: with staff and her friends at the hostel; with others who were living in supported flats; with a local authority social worker. Later, she was introduced to a worker from a housing association and spent some time with that association. The pursuit of choice and the assessment of needs went hand-in-hand. Eventually, she was able to obtain the tenancy of a small flat to share with a friend and with a 'package' of support from the housing association and from other sources to suit her particular circumstances.

We shall be looking in more detail later, and throughout this book, at the assessment and care planning process of Gladys and others. We will first, however, consider a more general framework for determining good practice.

	1. Readiness	2. Suitability	3. Opportunities
Aims	To assess readiness for change	To assess suitability for new situation	To explore opportunities for change
Focus	Performance	Adaptation	Potential
Instruments	Check-lists	Tests	Schedules
Criteria	Dependency level	Needs and available support	Quality of life
Options	To move on when ready	To be accepted if suitable	To explore all possibilities
Outcome evaluation	Did client move when ready?	Was client accepted if suitable?	Was appropriate support available

Figure 2 Types of approaches to assessment

As part of our research into assessment and resource allocation, we studied in detail what happened to 41 people in different locations in Scotland over a period of time when they were being assessed for a possible move. We found, as would be expected, very varied practices as well as attitudes to assessment. These seemed to cluster around three main types of approaches to assessment. The first we called the 'readiness' approach; the second the 'suitability' approach; the third the 'opportunities' approach. An outline of the features and implications of these approaches are set out in Figure 2.

The research was looking at overall or 'global' assessments required to determine whether clients should move from their present accommodation and, if so, where and with what support. The typology is therefore geared to these kinds of assessments. However, in general terms it is also applicable to programme assessments where one wants to analyse tasks, set targets or goals and develop appropriate training programmes.

The three types of approaches were found across a wide range of different kinds of moves that were being contemplated: for example, from hospitals to staffed houses; from staffed houses to un-staffed supported housing; from family care to residential care or supported accommodation; or for decisions about future living arrangements for young people leaving residential special schools.

The readiness approach

This approach is dominated by the idea of gradation or levels. There are levels of ability (or disability); of independence (or dependence). 'Levels' of dependency (or whatever) are assumed to be directly related to 'levels of provision' (for example staffing levels). Readiness relates to possible movement upwards, in the case of people with learning disabilities; but it is sometimes assumed to be downwards in the case of people with regressive conditions. Assessment is focused on the stage the client is at in relation to a classified system of conditions: for example, high, medium or low dependency. These conditions are typically expressed in quantitative rather than qualitative terms (i.e., a low, medium or high *amount* of support, or sometimes in terms of a score on a scale).

Applied to a person in a hospital, the question is whether the assessed level of dependency requires them to remain there or whether they are 'ready' to move into the community. Applied to an elderly person at risk with, say, dementia, living at home, the question is whether they are too dependent to remain outside hospital or other staffed establishment.

This approach to assessment tends to focus on the client's observed performance. This may be recorded using check-lists to determine how well tasks can be performed or situations handled. In some cases, this type of assessment will be carried out in a special setting, such as a trial flat or half-way house, recognising the limited opportunities available in settings such as a hospital ward, or even a hostel, for a valid assessment. One cannot, for example, assess whether a client could manage to boil an egg and make toast if they are denied the opportunity to try to do this.

Typically, this kind of assessment will be used to determine whether a client should move on to do something other than what he or she is doing currently, or move out from present accommodation to greater independence. In other words, it is informative about readiness to move, or to change something, but not so helpful in specific terms concerning where or what to change to. Its focus tends to be limited to an assessment 'out' or away from something, rather than an assessment for specific alternatives. The most to be expected is that it will offer some guidance about the level of support a client will require, with the implication that this would be in a particular type of accommodation.

The 'readiness' approach incorporates assumptions which are not sustainable in the light of recent research and practice experience. In particular, it should be noted:

- Dependency can be perpetuated by lack of opportunity

- There is not necessarily an association between levels of dependency and levels of provision

- Dependency is not necessarily associated with disability. (For example, a relatively able person might make heavier demands on staff because they are attempting to do more ambitious things.)

- Qualitative aspects of dependency may be more significant than quantitative measurements (see Chapter Eight).

The suitability approach

The suitability approach focuses on assessment to start a given programme, or to move to a particular placement. Its focus is an assessment 'in'. It is an assessment for reception. For example, in our research, a new purpose-built project was being developed to house people with learning disabilities in a cluster of different sized units: mostly flats for two people living together, but some single flats and one unit for four. From possible referrals, clients were being assessed for their suitability for one or another of the flats.

The suitability type of assessment focuses on social adaptation and possible social affiliations as well as on client performance. In the example given, the assessment was designed to inform the organisation providing the accommodation not only about levels of support that would be needed but also about which of the referred clients might adapt to living with others, who would benefit from living on their own, and so on.

Double assessments

Our research found that clients who moved from one type of accommodation to another were frequently assessed twice. First they were assessed for their 'readiness' to move out and then, quite separately, they were assessed for their 'suitability' for an alternative placement. For example:

> Jane had been making progress at a hostel run by a voluntary society. She wanted to be more independent. An assessment carried out at the hostel, based on a 'readiness' approach, confirmed her ability to live more independently. She was, therefore, referred to a large housing association where the process of assessment was repeated, only this time using a 'suitability' approach. As a result of the second assessment she was allocated to a particular house.

Double assessments are wasteful. Sometimes the practice occurs because different organisations are involved at each stage. In the case of Jane, the housing association felt it could not rely on the assessment provided by the voluntary home. In any case, the 'readiness' approach to assessment would not provide the kind of detailed information the receiving agency would need to decide where Jane should be placed.

The research showed that sometimes a single more comprehensive type of assessment could be carried out with the involvement of different agencies.

The practice of care management should remove the traditional tendency to separate assessed 'readiness' for something from 'suitability' for something. Organisationally, the responsibility for a unified assessment procedure lies with the purchaser acting with the client.

The opportunities approach

The 'opportunities' type of assessment has a broader perspective than either of the other two approaches. At the same time, it points to more specific programme or placement plans.

The aims of this type of assessment are exploratory – that is to explore with the client the best ways forward. This implies an open-ended view of future possibilities. The focus is on potential – both the potential of the client and of informal carers and the potential of support services. We referred earlier to the example of Gladys:

> Gladys was encouraged to think through with a variety of people what she wanted for the future and what the implications for support would be. For example, if she moved into a proposed flat, would she be able to continue her part-time work? How would she get to work? What help would she need in the new situation if she moved?

Thus the emphasis is on support rather than performance. It is on potential rather than adaptation. The criteria on which the assessment is based relate to an overall quality of life rather than a view of the client as a 'dependent' who might or might not be 'suitable' for a given service.

Quality of life criteria

The research provided evidence that, based on quality of life criteria, the 'opportunities' approach was associated with better placement outcomes. What, however, does 'quality of life' mean?

A Canadian community care researcher, Robert Schalock (1989), suggests that 'quality of life' is replacing such ideas as 'normalisation' and 'de- institutionalisation' as the main force for change.

'Quality of life' encompasses wellbeing in terms of both the inner self and the environment. It implies that one should aim for people to be happy within themselves, but not at the expense of others and not at the expense of the environment. It implies a safe and protected environment.

For all of us, the environment has many components, from the facilities of the rooms we occupy and the location of our dwelling, to the air we breathe, the food we eat, the friends we have and how accessible they are, and our safety and security. An assessment based on quality of life criteria will address all of these issues, as well as the difficulties, support needs and potential of the individual.

Schalock and his colleagues suggest three kinds of indicators of a good quality of life: social indicators, psychological indicators and social policy indicators. Drawing together these three approaches they go on to suggest a quality of life index with three groupings of factor scores.

> Factor 1 is headed 'environmental control' and includes such questions as:
>
> • How many people sleep in your bedroom?
> • Do you decide when to get up and when to go to bed?
> • Who plans your meals?
>
> Factor 2 is headed 'community involvement' and includes questions about work, transport and use of recreational activities.
>
> Factor 3 is headed 'social relations' and includes questions about neighbours, friends, the locality as well as, for example, 'Do you have any pets?'

Other writers have suggested other frameworks which are reviewed in another publication arising from our research (Seed 1992). These different frameworks share the recognition that assessment encompasses:

1. Individual opportunities based on choice

2. Support and facilities to make use of these opportunities

3. Health and safety.

These criteria were applied to Gladys's move from a hostel to a flat of her choice. In other words, assessment addressed the following:

1. What does Gladys want? What opportunities are there for her to obtain what she wants? (In Gladys' case, she wanted to live with a friend in a flat.)

2. What support will Gladys need to take advantage of these opportunities? Who can provide it?

3. What are the particular implications of any health problems and how can her positive health be promoted in a new environment? Are there any particular health or safety hazards that have to be addressed?

The quality of life approach to assessment converges with the principles of good practice deduced from our research which were listed in the last chapter.

Assessment instruments

We have begun the discussion of assessment with types of approaches and attitudes to assessment rather than with descriptions of instruments. This is deliberate. It is our experience that community care professionals tend to start with an instrument, or with the search for one, and we suggest this is not the right place to start.

Whatever assessment instrument is used, the attitude to its use is likely to be more influential for the assessment than the instrument itself. The most sophisticated assessment instrument might be based on global quality of life criteria. It would be largely wasted if those using it saw it only as an instrument to measure 'readiness' or 'suitability'.

An assessment instrument can serve extraneous functions for the community care organisation. Evidence from various research projects with which we have been associated points to a tendency for a staff team to use an instrument as something to invest in to sustain the team's identity.

James Hogg and Norma Raynes (1987), with reference to their review of assessments in the field of learning disabilities states:

> The importance of assessment to those providing services is reflected not only in the development of tests of the kind described in this volume, but also in the extent to which professionals have devised their own assessment procedures for individual schools, adult training centres, hospitals and residential establishments... (p.10)

The state of assessment is not so well advanced that such efforts should be decried, though hopefully we look to a future in which appropriate and sound tests will be available making the need for such individual initiatives less pressing...

Because an assessment device has been developed to meet local needs, and because it induces a feeling of familiarity and comfort in the service provider cum test deviser, these facts do not mean it is an adequate or acceptable test by the criterion of good test construction.

The idea of gradually moving towards a single authentic assessment instrument has some attractions. However, there are difficulties. It is our view that we should get away from the notion of a global assessment in community care as being any kind of 'test' at all. It is an exploration of opportunities undertaken with the client and of the support service implications.

Here is a simple example of the difference between a test and an exploration of opportunities:

Test Question	Exploration Question
Can the client walk independently to a bus-stop, hail a bus, recognise the route, tender his/her fare and state the destination?	Is a bus-service available to enable the client to travel and, if so, does he/she need support or assistance to board the bus?

Having said that we favour an exploratory approach for global assessments, we recognise that an element of testing is incorporated in specific programme assessments for evaluating progress towards agreed goals. Such programmes should be agreed within a general exploratory framework.

For example, supposing the answer for Mr Smith to the exploratory question above is that he has a bus service which he could use to reach a day centre, that he can reach the bus stop unaccompanied, but that he cannot tell which bus to hail. The day centre might then concentrate on a training programme designed to help him to recognise his bus by the number on the destination board. This becomes a training goal. An assessment to determine, after a given period, whether this goal has been attained may be regarded in some ways as a 'test'. But the 'test' is limited to a highly specific situation. We are not generalising the test to produce inferences for levels of ability or of anything else.

Validity and reliability

Questions of validity and reliability need to be addressed in any formal procedures which will be adopted for exploratory as well as for test purposes.

The validity question is whether the instrument or procedure addresses the issues it needs to address in order to fulfil the purposes it claims. In the example above, does the way the exploratory question is constructed adequately address the issue it is intended to address? The reliability issue is whether, in the hands of different assessors, similar answers would be obtained. Reliability is especially important when scoring is incorporated in the procedure. Scoring serves to give a simplified meaning to what would otherwise be a long list of unconnected pieces of information.

Data gathering and recording

In considering assessment procedures, we should distinguish between the processes of gathering information and recording it. In other words, if a data recording instrument covers a long list of issues about support needs or existing services or about personal or health background, it does not follow that the person assessing has necessarily to sit down with the client and formally address each item if the information is already well known. On the other hand, information that is thought to be well known should be checked with the client before the assessment record is completed.

Information about client wishes and intentions may often be gathered most effectively in group discussions, especially in residential and day service settings. This is partly because some clients will be more confident in groups, and group discussions will help to clarify their own personal preferences. It is also because what the client wants may be bound up in practical terms with what the group wants – perhaps, better food, more opportunities to shop or similar things. But where the issues affect the individual client alone, he or she should be seen individually. For example:

> Beth lived in an old house in a large city with eight others. The group view, which had become the agency policy, was that the house should be closed and the residents dispersed. This was problem for Beth because, although she had not said

so in the group, she was quite content to stay. Of course, in this kind of group situation, not everyone could be equally satisfied. Yet it was only when Beth was seen individually that her particular feelings emerged and could be addressed.

Ideally, the instruments for data recording – schedule, question-naire, diaries or whatever – should involve different people in the processes of data gathering. For example, if the data recording instrument to determine the wishes of the residents in Beth's case had been a questionnaire, it would not be sufficient simply to give each resident a form to fill in by themselves. It is also, as we have said, insufficient to rely solely on a group discussion. Ideally, there should be a range of processes and procedures to ensure that the most reliable and valid information is gathered.

A DEMONSTRATION ASSESSMENT INSTRUMENT

During the early stages of our research we could not find any existing assessment instrument which (i) adequately catered for all the points we have made about the approach required for care in the community and which (ii) allowed for the necessary follow-through from assessment to care management. We therefore de-vised and developed our own comprehensive instrument. The instrument has been further developed in a range of other research and assessment projects.

We will be dealing with the question of the care management follow-through from assessment (for example in terms of service costing, resource allocation and planning procedures) in later chap-ters. At this stage, we shall describe the uses of the Demonstration Instrument in terms of the assessment part of the process.

The Demonstration Instrument has fourteen parts altogether, but only six of these relate to the initial exploration of opportunities based on quality of life criteria. These parts deal with:

1. Personal information, social background and health

2. Client views and preferences

3. Support needs and resource implications

4. Main carer's perspective

5. Review of existing formal support services

6. Review of existing informal support.

Two further parts monitor existing services and informal support in greater detail. These comprise:

7. Support staff diaries

8. Client diaries.

Both sets of diaries are kept for concurrent periods of 14 days.

The remaining parts 9–14 (as well as some sections within parts 5–6) deal with service costing, planning, evaluation and other aspects of care management.

Information about me . . . . (Name) to help to
 plan for the future

When completed . . . . (Date)

This part is completed by . . . . (. . . . .)*

 with help from . . . . (. . . . .)*

* State position e.g. resident, key worker, care manager

---

*Figure 3 Format for introductory sheet of each part of the demonstration
 assessment instrument*

Each part has a similar introductory format (see Figure 3). This underscores what we have said about information-gathering being a shared process. We want to know not only whom the information is about but who helped whom in providing it. A second point to note is the use of the word 'I' rather than 'you' in referring to the person being assessed. This has generally been found to be acceptable and of some possible advantage in emphasising that the right to the ownership of the assessment should belong to the person being assessed. It is made available to the service purchaser or providers with the consent of the person assessed (i.e., the client). In other words, we are endeavouring to help the client to feel: 'This is my assessment of aspects of my life which you are helping me with in order that I can have better services from you' rather than 'I, the professional, am assessing you to see what you want and need'.

1. Personal details, social background and health

Apart from personal data comprising name, gender, date of birth, address and so forth, the first section deals with the client's social setting:

Description of accommodation ....
....
....
....

Description of neighbourhood............................
....
....
....

Who else (if anyone) shares the accommodation with the client?
   Name   *Relationship to client (if any)*
   ....
   ....

Other relatives or close friends currently in close contact:
   Name   *Relationship to client (if any)*
   ....
   ....

Client's access to car or other transport (*describe situation*) ....
....
....
....

Access to key community facilities (*e.g. post office, doctor's surgery, essential shopping*) ....
....
....
....

For practitioner (rather than research) purposes, we favour the use of 'open prompts' rather than 'closed questions' wherever possible. (This is the difference between a 'schedule' and a 'questionnaire'.) For example, we ask for 'details of accommodation' rather than a fixed list of closed questions such as: 'How many bedrooms? Bathrooms? and so on'. This is to avoid unnecessary detail and to allow the kind of data to emerge which are significant in the particular instance. For example, the fact that a blind and disabled person lived in a house at the top of steep hill, approached by a long flight of steps or that the house had four rooms on three different levels, would be more significant than the number of bedrooms.

There are, however, instances when a standard format for specific closed questions is required, as in the next section which gives the essential information usually needed about the client's previous history:

History of previous accommodation:

Moved from	*To*	*When*
. . . .	. . . .	. . . .
. . . .	. . . .	. . . .

History of schooling:

Moved from	*To*	*When*
. . . .	. . . .	. . . .
. . . .	. . . .	. . . .

Other history since leaving school (*eg. work, training, FE courses etc*)

Moved from	*To*	*When*
. . . .	. . . .	. . . .
. . . .	. . . .	. . . .

More specific information about the past may be useful in particular circumstances. For example, when assessing the needs of people in residential establishments it is helpful to include:

How old was I when I left my parent's home? . . . .
. . . .
. . . .

Are my mother/father/other family alive? . . . .
. . . .

(If alive) When do I see them? . . . .
. . . .
. . . .

The amount of detail in the format will, again, depend on the circumstances. If the schedule is intended to be completed, for example, by a person with learning disabilities it will be helpful to separate out the questions for mother, father, brother(s), sister(s) and so on.

The final section in this part concerns a health and sensory assessment. The following format for health issues has been well used in a large number of assessments for different client groups:

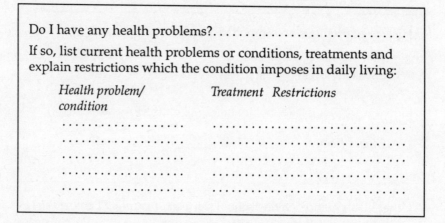

Do I have any health problems?...............................
If so, list current health problems or conditions, treatments and explain restrictions which the condition imposes in daily living:

Health problem/   Treatment Restrictions
condition

....
....
....
....
....

A further question is included for past health problems which still impose current restrictions. For example, one completed form from the research lists a broken leg as a past problem which required a knee and leg pin. Although this was in the past, the current restriction was that the client could not walk far and had a tendency to fall unless supported.

Sensory issues are sometimes overlooked in social assessments and we think these are basic to community care. The Instrument therefore includes specific questions on eyesight, hearing, smell, and allows space for other senses. The format allows for sensory perception to be noted which is exceptionally good as well as poor. For example:

Is my eyesight:

Exceptionally good

Normal

Poor

Partially impaired

Total impairment (totally blind)

Not known

Do I wear glasses? ....

....

When was my eyesight last tested? ....

....

If my eyesight is exceptionally good, give an example of the
circumstances where this is shown ....

....

....

2. Client views and preferences

Client views are likely to be more reliably gathered and recorded
in the context of factual information related to these views. For
example, the first section of this part of the Demonstration Instrument, which deals with views about present accommodation, asks
first a general question 'What generally do I feel about where I am
living?' and then goes on to the following detail:

How many residents are there altogether in this house?
Is this:

(a) Just the right number of people I like to live with 1

(b) Too few people. I would like to be with more people 2

(c) Too many people. I would like to be with fewer
people 3

(d) Don't know 4

(e) Other answers (state): 9

Do I have a room to myself?. . . . .

   If NO, how many others sleep in my room? . . . .

If I share my room:

   Are these the people I like to share my room with? . . . .

   Would I prefer to share a room with someone else? . . . .

   Would I prefer not to have to share a room at all? . . . .

If I have a room to myself:

   Do I like sleeping in a room by myself? . . . .

   Would I prefer to share a room with someone? . . . .

      If so, explain why: . . . .

      . . . .

Can I keep people out of my room if I don't want them to come in?

. . . .

Can I get into my own room any time I want to? . . . .

Can I decide what I can keep in my room and where to put it?

   Eg. Pictures on the walls? . . . .

   What furniture to have?. . . . .

Do I feel safe when I am in my room?. . . . .

Do I ever feel frightened when I am in my room? . . . .

   If 'frightened', explain why: . . . .

   . . . .

In general, do I like my room?*

   I like it very much. 1

   I don't like it very much 2

   I don't feel one way or the other about it 3

   Don't know 4

   Other answers (state): 9

* Circle the number by the answer and add comments below

What, if anything, would improve my room?: . . . .

. . . .

There are several points to note about this kind of format. First, as we have said, a question about fact is followed by questions about views upon the fact. 'Do I share a room ?' (Fact) 'Would I prefer not to have to share a room?' (Preference). Second, questions are varied in such a way as to allow for a consistent pattern to emerge from 'Yes' and 'No' to different items. This variation is important for the reliability of answers where clients may not easily understand all the questions or may have a tendency always to say 'yes' (or perhaps 'no') to every question. Third, it will be noted that the data gathered serve the dual purposes of (i) reflecting on the present accommodation and (ii) giving information of value in considering future accommodation possibilities.

The next section concerns food and shopping:

Are meals provided? ....

Do I get the chance to make my own meals or snacks? ....

....

    If YES, does anybody help me? ....

        Who helps me? .... (Position.........)

Do I get enough help? ....

....

Do people help me too much sometimes? ....

....

Would I rather make my own meals without so much help? ......

....

Do I get the chance to choose my own food?...................

....

Would I like the chance to choose my own food more often?.....

....

Do I do my own shopping? ....

    If YES, what sorts of things do I especially like to buy?.......

....

Are there things I would like to buy but don't get the chance to go to the right shops? Explain where I would like to go? ....

....

....

Do I get enough help with shopping?. . . . .
. . . .
Do people help me too much sometimes? . . . .
. . . .
Would I rather do my own shopping sometimes without so much
help?. . . . .
. . . .

The questions then go on to generalise from shopping to other
activities and opportunities outside the house. For example:

Do I get opportunities to make new friends?. . . . .
. . . .
What opportunities are these? . . . .
. . . .
Do I get enough help to make new friends?. . . . .
. . . .
Do I sometimes get too much help from people who want me to
make friends? If YES, explain: . . . .
. . . .

This part of the assessment concludes, as it began, with some
general questions:

Would I like to stay at this house during the next few years,
perhaps if some things could be improved?
    If NO, would I like to move somewhere else?. . . . .
. . . .
    Where to? What sort of place? . . . .
. . . .
    If YES, what, if any, improvements would I like to see?. . . . . . .
. . . .

The wording of this part was designed to be answered, with help, by people with learning disabilities. There could be some modification of the formulation, perhaps, for some other client groups. The wording is also specifically geared to people in residential or other supported accommodation. It should, however, be able to be used in this form for people living in their own accommodation or with parents or other relatives.

Having someone to help with the gathering of views, and the information related to these views, allows for further explanations to be recorded and also allows the user to skip through sections which have no direct application to the particular situation being assessed. For example, if a person lives by themselves, the questions about other residents and sharing rooms can be skipped.

3. Support needs

This part of the Instrument has evolved through many years of research and application to practice in relation to people with learning disabilities and with other groups.

The evolution reflects the changes in attitudes to assessment discussed at the beginning of this chapter. Originally, when used in research in the Highlands and Islands of Scotland as an instrument for assessing the needs of people (of all ages) with learning disabilities, the heading 'Levels of Performance' was adopted. Later, to get away from a quantitative measure of 'levels' to qualitative aspects, it was headed 'Features of Performance'. Finally, in response to comments from a colleague, Fiona Harkess, the heading was changed to 'Support Needs'. In other words, the object of the exercise is not to test and measure performance but to explore needs in a given social situation.

The Instrument looks at a number of key situations in personal care and daily living. These are:

- Personal care – getting dressed
  - washing, bathing and toilet
  - eating and drinking
- Daily living – communication
  - getting about (mobility)
  - preparing a meal
  - keeping room/house tidy and clean

- reading and writing
- using public transport
- managing money
- support with hobbies etc
- support in work (paid or voluntary).

Other situations could be substituted, depending on the use to which the Instrument is put. For example, understanding the time has been included when the Instrument has been used with children.

There is a standard format of questions and prompts for each social situation. Figure 4 shows this format for the situation of getting dressed. The key question is:

Do I need assistance or support? ....
....

If the answer is 'No – I manage fine myself', there is no need for further investigation. One moves quickly on to the next situation. (This can be a very time-saving procedure compared with using check-lists.)

If the answer is 'Yes' and either 'sometimes' or 'always' a description is called for of the precise sticking points or difficulties and of the support and/or assistance required. Some prompts are given as to likely difficulties (for example buttons, zips, shoes in the case of dressing), but these are only illustrations. The range of different aspects of the question are also explained (for example deciding what to wear, when to change, knowing what is appropriate and so forth).

'Assistance' and 'support' are distinguished and defined. 'Assistance' means 'hands on' physical assistance – in this example, perhaps putting shoes on, helping to tie a tie, or suchlike. 'Support' means encouragement to manage to do these things, or perhaps supervision or instruction. The two kinds of help can be independent of each other. A client might need assistance but not support, support but not assistance, or both.

1. Do I need *assistance* and/or *support* to get dressed?*
   (This includes deciding what to wear, knowing when to change, knowing what is appropriate for different occasions and weather or, for some actually getting dressed or undressed.

   * *Assistance* means actual (physical) help
     Support means encouragement by someone being there

	Assistance	Support
No, I manage fine myself	1	1
Yes, but only sometimes	2	2
I do not get the chance to find out if I can manage by myself	3	3
Yes, I do need support and/or assistance always	4	4

   * Circle the numbers beside the answer, or write the answer below:

   If I have circled 1 and can manage fine by myself, there is no need to write anything more here.

   If I have circled one of the other numbers for one of the other answers, please explain what *assistance* and/or *support* are *needed* and exactly what they are needed for. Say how much I can do myself.

   State what the sticking points are:

   e.g. buttons, zips, shoes. If help is needed with most things, state in what ways I can or cannot co-operate with the person getting me dressed. . . . .
   . . . .
   . . . .
   . . . .

   Is more help needed to learn to do these things better? What else is needed? (Include time, more people to help or any equipment.)
   . . . .
   . . . .
   . . . .

Figure 4 Specimen question from Part 3 – support needs

The question asks for a specification of the kinds of assistance/support needed and then asks:

Is more help needed to learn to do this better? . . . .
What else is needed? . . . .
. . . .
. . . .
(Include time, more people to help, or any equipment.)

This is not a format which is sufficient in itself to develop a training programme. It does help to indicate where such a programme is called for, or may require changing if already in existence. It also provides a framework for evaluating the results of any such programme in everyday living. For example, if tasks relating to dressing were broken down to form a programme of training for a young person with multiple disabilities, the relevance and the success of such a programme could be evaluated partly with reference to the answers given in this part of the Instrument.

There is also an open question at the end of the section:

What things, out of all these questions, or other things not
mentioned, have I learnt to do better for myself during the past
year that I could not do a year ago?. . . . .
. . . .
Is there anything that I used to be able to do a year ago that I can't
do so well now without more assistance or support?. . . . .
    If 'Yes' what things can I not do so well now?. . . . .
. . . .
. . . .

It is, as we have said, assumed that the schedule is completed jointly by the client and the person responsible for the assessment. (In some cases we have left the schedule with the client and discussed the answers with him or her subsequently.) A further question at the end asks:

When completing this form, was there any disagreement between myself and the person helping me to answer these questions? . . .
. . . .
Explain what, if anything, I disagreed about: . . . .
. . . .
. . . .
. . . .

We have talked about reliability, in terms of ensuring that similar answers would be given if different people were involved in completing the assessment. This issue is not to be confused with different answers being given about the same client for similar tasks, but in different situations – for example, at home, at work, at a day centre or in a residential establishment. Different but equally valid and reliable answers may well be given if the questions are asked with respect to different settings, and the differences will be important to note. For example, a client may be able to do some things with less support at home that at a day centre, or vice versa. The implications of differences may be that, first, they should be made known and second, the reasons sought.

4. Main carer's perspective

This part of the Instrument was designed for use in cases where the client is not living with the carer. A different set of questions is required where the carer is at home with the client.

The initial questions deal with the carer's own home circumstances (including their health) and the distance they live away from the client. There are then questions about frequency of visits and any transport problems.

Would you visit him/her more often if these problems were overcome? . . . .
Are there any transport problems in the resident visiting you? . . . .
. . . .
    If YES, explain: . . . .
. . . .
Do you think he/she would visit more often if these problems were overcome? . . . .
. . . .

How do his/her visits affect other members of your family living
at home?..
....
Does it cause you stress when you meet... (resident)? ....
....
    If YES, explain: ....
....

Does it cause stress to any other members of your family when
they meet... (resident)?.......................................
    If YES, explain: ....
....

The instrument then asks for carer's views about various aspects
of the resident's present accommodation: staffing, food, opportunities and other features the carer may wish to single out.

Taking all this into account, do you think the resident should
remain where he/she is or move somewhere else? ....
....
If 'move somewhere else' what things would you think it
important to take into account? ....
....
If the reply is 'to remain' do you have any further comments on
what might be provided? ....
....

If he/she were to move, how would this affect you or others on
the household? In what ways?................................
....

An adaptation of this part of the Instrument to carers of clients at
home includes the following specific questions:

Thinking about the future: what additional kinds of assis-
tance/support do you think are needed (a) soon, (b) in the longer
term? For example:

(i) Long-term residential care in the near future

(ii) Long-term care, not immediately or in the near future but
perhaps in a few years' time

(iii) Just knowing that if anything should happen (to me) a
place in a residential home would be available

(iv) Additional support to enable... (client) to remain at home
should anything happen to me

and/or:

(v) Periodic respite care

(vi) Holiday respite

(vii) Respite at week-ends

(viii) Respite in emergencies

(ix) Other (specify)

This adapted form was used, together with other parts of the
Instrument, to assess the needs of families in a particular area, at
the request of a carers' group. This led to a long-term residential
house and a respite facility being established through a voluntary
organisation in which the carers and clients participated.

The gathering of information about carers' views does not, of
course, imply that they should take precedence over clients' views.
There may be conflicts between the two; knowing about carers'
views is necessary to identify where such conflicts, as well as
congruence and sources of support, exist. These issues are discussed further in Chapter Three.

5. Review of existing formal support services

The front sheet of this part establishes a global picture of social
services and other formal support services the client or client and
carer (in the case of people living at home) receive. Figure 5 shows
an example of this sheet for clients with multiple disabilities – it
would be to some extent varied for other groups to avoid a very
long check-list intended to cover everything that anyone might
conceivably receive.

5.1 Which of the following special services have I received from outside this house during the past 12 months? Include visiting services and services where I go elsewhere. 'Special services' means services to meet special needs. They do not therefore include normal use of the NHS or use of normal educational or recreational services but they do include special support to make use of normal services.

At:

Training/support for work . . . . 1 . . . .
Support for leisure facilities . . . . 2 . . . .
Further education (Special needs) . . . . 3 . . . .
Home help . . . . 4 . . . .
SSD day service . . . . 5 . . . .
Other specialist day service . . . . 6 . . . .
Psychologist . . . . 7 . . . .
Physiotherapy . . . . 8 . . . .
Occupational therapy . . . . 9 . . . .
Speech therapy . . . . 10 . . . .
Community nurse . . . . 11 . . . .
Drama therapy . . . . 12 . . . .
Music therapy . . . . 13 . . . .
Respite . . . . 14 . . . .
Other special holiday . . . . 15 . . . .
Other (state) . . . . 16 . . . .
Other (state) . . . . 17 . . . .
Other (state) . . . . 18 . . . .

It may be useful to use this list to sort out where different services are provided (*e.g. at a day centre, college, at home, etc.*)

Figure 5 Format for front sheet to part 5: formal support services

The next sets of sheets allow for more detailed assessment of key services. We usually put a maximum on the number of services to be included (three to five). For each service, we then ask for details of the agency and personnel involved in service delivery, how the client came to use the service (at whose suggestion?) and statements of the purposes and objectives of the service for the client both in the past and now:

What is the objective now? . . . .
. . . .
When was the need for this service last reviewed? . . . .
. . . .
Who was involved in the review? . . . .
. . . .
Was the report of this review made available to me? To my Carer? To my keyworker? . . . .
. . . .
What were the recommendations of this review so far as I was concerned? Was each of these recommendations carried out? If not, explain why...

Recommendations:	Carried out: (Yes/No/Partly)	Reason: (If not carried out)
. . . .	. . . .	. . . .
. . . .	. . . .	. . . .
. . . .	. . . .	. . . .

How much longer is this service likely to be available? . . . .
. . . .
How useful is this service for me? . . . .
. . . .

	Staff view	My view
Essential	1	1
Useful but not essential	2	2
Not very useful or helpful	3	3
Not useful/helpful at all	4	4
Other answers	9	9

Explain any disagreements between staff and myself about this service. . . . .
. . . .

Staff diary   Name of Staff . . . .
                     Name of Client. . . . .

This diary has two purposes. The first is to estimate staff time spent with individual residents. The second is to complement client diaries in identifying key activities in daily living related to support requirements. *Please complete separate sheet for each client for each day for a fortnight.*

Time:	Event or Activity	No. of residents involved	No. of staff involved	Staff time with this resident see code below
To 7.0am				
To 8.0				
To 9.0				
To 10.0				
To 11.0				
To Noon				
To 1.0				
To 2.0				
To 3.0				
To 4.0				
To 5.0				
To 6.0				
To 7.0				
To 8.0				
To 9.0				
From 10.0pm				

Code for the last column:

A = 1:1 attention with this resident

B = Less than 1:1 but more time than with other residents in the group during this activity

C = Average time compared with others during this activity

D = Less time than for other residents during this activity

E = Requires no staff time at all during this activity

F = Other answers (explain)

Figure 6 Format for the staff diary

Other sections of this part of the Instrument deal with estimated service costs. These will be outlined and discussed in Chapter Six.

6. Review of informal support

This part covers activities or events not included in formal services. This could, for example, include clubs, help from neighbours or informal voluntary services or arrangements. For each important source of support, details are asked about the activity, who the client is with, frequency and regularity and which, if any, staff are involved.

The same format is then used as for formal services to ask for staff and client views on whether the support is essential, useful or not helpful. Again, costing data is obtained (see Chapter Six).

7. Support staff diaries

The format for this diary is shown in Figure 6. It will be seen that it is addressed to staff, although clients should be aware that it is taking place. It serves to monitor how staff spend their time with the particular client we are concerned with in the context of demands from other clients in a residential setting. In a slightly modified form, it is also suitable for monitoring the use of day-service time.

Apart from the data the diary gives for service costing, it can be used to reveal in graphic form the pattern of staffing required to meet the support needs of an individual client and which activities take up most or least time. This is illustrated in the example shown in Figure 7. The pattern of staffing demands will have implications for future staffing needs in the light of data from other parts of the assessment, especially the part dealing with support needs.

8. Client diaries

These give life and context to everything else included. They provide direct evidence of activities and events which can be represented as a network diagram helping to illuminate key features relevant to assessing quality of life.

Details of the philosophy, background and technicalities as well as of the potential use of such diaries are described in detail in *Introducing Network Analysis in Social Work* (Seed 1990).

They have been now used in a large range of practice situations as well as for research purposes, and their usefulness vindicated in most cases. An exception was a recent trial with carers of people

Summary of 24-hour periods showing clusters of hours of
the day during a fortnight when a client needed more (or
less) time than other residents.

Time   *Pattern of time*

To				
7.0 am				E
8.0		BBBBB CCC		
9.0		CCC	DDDD	
10.0				E
11.0				E
12. Noon				E
1.0 pm		BBBBB CCC		E
2.0				E
3.0				E
4.0				E
5.0	AAAAAAAAAAAAA	BBBBB		
6.0	AAAAAAAAAAAAA	BBBBB		
7.0		BBBBB CCCC		
8.0	AA	CCCC	DDDDDDDD	E
9.0	AA	BBBBBB CC	DDDDDD	
10.0				E
11.0 and after				

Code:

A = 1:1 attention with this resident

B = Less than 1:1 but more time than with other residents in
    the group during this activity

C = Average time compared with others during this activity

D = Less time than for other residents during this activity

E = Requires no staff time at all during this activity

F = Other answers (explain)

Figure 7 Display of data produced from completed staff diaries

with dementia, since it appeared to cause the carers additional
anxiety. However, this was exceptional in that the application was
to carers rather than to clients. The diaries are designed to record
the patterns of daily living of clients with help from carers, where
required, in completing them. In these circumstances they do not
appear to cause carers the same anxiety as might be the case if they
were their own diaries.

Daily Diary for .... For (day) .... (date) ....

What happened today?	List events or activities at home:	Who were you with? If lots of people, name the important ones. Explain who the people are (*e.g. brother, friend, etc.*)
During the morning		
During the afternoon		
During the evening or night		

Did you go out anywhere today?

	Places visited	Who with	How did you travel	Event or activity	Who else did you meet?
All day: **or morning or afternoon or evening or night**					

Did anything happen today that you want to comment on further? ....

Additional comments from person who assisted in completing diary (if applicable) ....
....

Figure 8 Standard format for client's daily diary

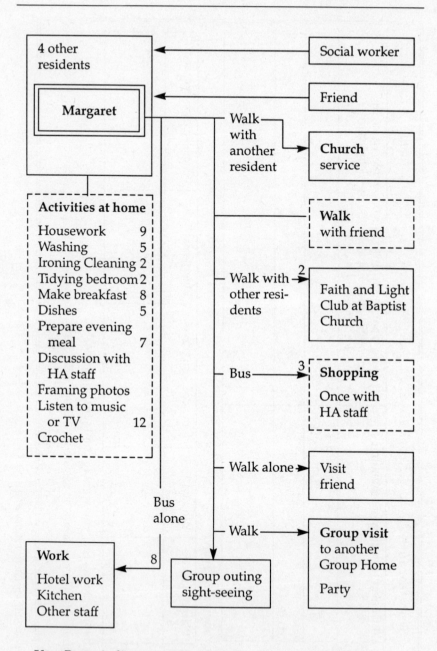

Key: Boxes indicate significant places. Numbers indicate frequency of visits in or out from home (top left). Activities are included in broken boxes

Figure 9 Network produced from diaries – 14 days in the life of Margaret

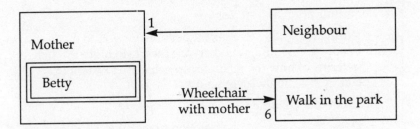

This and the previous illustration (Figure 9) are fictitious but based on real examples

Key: Boxes indicate significant places. Numbers indicate frequency of visits in or out from home (top left)

Figure 10 Contrasting network produced from diaries – 14 days in the life of Betty

Slightly different diary formats can be used in different settings and circumstances. A standard format for general use is reproduced in Figure 8. Two contrasting networks showing the patterns of living for a fortnight based on these diaries for two different clients are shown in Figures 9 and 10.

The diaries are, of course, used in conjunction with the other parts of the Instrument. In the case of assessing a client living at home it is usual to complete Parts 1–3 of the Instrument during an initial interview, leave the diary forms and complete Parts 4–6 when the diaries are collected after the agreed period of a fortnight has elapsed.

Relationship qualities

Diaries have been found to give reliable information about contacts but this needs to be supplemented by information about the quality of key relationships. We have systematised the assessment of key relationships in terms of what we call 'relationship qualities'. When completed diaries are collected, we ask the client (where necessary with help from the carer) to name up to three people regarded as the most important of all those mentioned in the diaries. We then ask a series of questions about each named person in turn. The precise wording of the question is less important than the sense of what is required below:

1. Communication and Access

  Does . . . . make it possible for you to meet other people you would not otherwise meet? (Explore the answer in terms of how the relationship helps the resident in communication with others).

2. Instrumental Qualities

  Does . . . . help you in practical ways. (For example, personal tasks or, perhaps, simply giving information)

3. Sentiments

  Apart from whether . . . . helps you in practical ways, how do you feel towards. . . . . ? (Explore possible feelings such as affection, friendship, fear, anger sometimes).

4. Influence

  Does . . . . influence you in particular ways, for example in deciding what you should do or how you should behave? In what sorts of ways? How do you feel about this?

5. Esteem

  Does . . . . treat you as he/she treats everyone else? Would you say he/she respects you?

6. Reciprocal Qualities

  Finally, can we look at this the other way round? What do you think. . . . . gains from you? How do they benefit from being with you?

Making use of the data

All of the information from the various parts of the assessment process – which we have suggested should be modelled on the lines of the Demonstration Instrument – has to be brought together in an intelligible form for care management purposes. In the remainder of this chapter we will outline a number of ways in which this is achieved.

Summary needs profile

This is a descriptive assessment on which care plans can be based. It produces a set of summaries, usually three to four pages in length. Figure 11 shows the format we have used for this purpose. The summary is accompanied by a network drawing based on the diaries where these have been kept. Where relevant and helpful, staff diaries displays (see Figure 7) will also be included.

Summary needs profile

Name of project: . . . .

Network reference: . . . .

Client's code-name . . . .

Summary headings:

    (A) Background and health

    (B) Social support needs

    (C) Interests, preferences and social network features

    (D) Present services

    (E) Implications and Growth Points

    (F) Agreed recommendations

Figure 11 Suggested format for summary needs profile

The idea of 'growth points' is to take the implications of (i) support needs and (ii) the potential of the social network together and to ask 'What next?' For example:

> Joe had been excluded from school because of behaviour problems. But, as he came up to school leaving, an individual programme had been arranged outside school with the assistance of volunteers, based on more adult activities. He had surprisingly shown a potential for concentration in an adult, rather than a children's, learning situation. A detailed assessment of his potential in different activities led to the identification of specific 'growth points'. These were addressed by his obtaining supported employment.

Needs profile for project development

Individual summaries along the lines described above are also used to develop a specific project – for example a day service or a residential or respite service – around the needs of a given group of clients. The following are some examples in which we have been involved, using the kind of Demonstration Instrument and needs profile described:

- Assessment of a group of hospital patients for accommodation in a village (Cornerstone Community Care)
- Assessment of family needs with reference to sons/daughters with severe or profound disabilities leaving home and settling in a house in the local community (Elgin Parents Group, Cornerstone).
- A parallel study to plan respite for parents of sons/daughters remaining at home (Elgin Parents Group, Cornerstone).
- A study of needs for a specialist day service for a young adults with profound and multiple disabilities in Dundee (White Top Project).
- A study of needs of children and adults with profound mental handicap for a specialist day service (Aveyron Parents Group, Hamilton and East Kilbride).
- A study of needs of a small group of adults with disabilities for planning a locally-based residential community (Scott Foundation, Kent).
- Needs assessments of people with head injuries (Headway, Tunbridge Wells).

The identification of individual 'growth-points' provides the initial focus for planning service needs. These are listed, together with the resource implications in terms of staffing, equipment, transport and other resources. Aggregation can then be made within each category and the implications summarised for

1. Buildings, including adaptations
2. Equipment and other capital items
3. Furnishing
4. Staffing

5. Other revenue items

6. Other services.

Other approaches to assessment for planning

An alternative approach to needs-led assessments for service planning is to adopt an entirely separate assessment procedure specifically for service planning. For example, with reference to people with dementia, a number of research projects are currently being sponsored by the Scottish Home and Health Department. These may be more appropriate than aggregating data from individual service profiles where we are concerned with larger-scale planning, for example on a regional basis (see Chapter Seven).

Computerised assessments

Computers can help with assessment in community care in two distinct respects:

1. Interactive computer programmes can assist with data gathering and recording. For example, a computer version of the Demonstration Instrument has been developed in prototype and trials have shown two advantages over a manual version. First, a menu-driven programme enables the user to move freely around the Instrument and to re- arrange groups of questions for this purpose. For example, all items related to shopping can be clustered from Part 2 (Client Views), Part 3 (Social support Needs) and Part 6 (Informal Support). Second, younger clients brought up and educated in a computer environment may take more readily to responding to questions on a computer than to using a manual procedure.

    There are several interactive computer programmes on the market which will also assist with programme assessment and planning (Rasmussen and Hersom 1987).

2. Computer programmes will assist with data analysis. This applies at the level of individual assessments and at the level of aggregating data for planning, monitoring or research purposes.

The authors, and colleagues from the Social Work and Micro-computing Centre at the University of Dundee are available for consultation on technical aspects of data analysis and computing.

CHAPTER THREE

Assessment and Client Choice

Respect for client choice is a principle of good assessment and care management. It is both a means to a sound assessment and an end in itself in the assessment and care management process.

At the beginning of the last chapter we claimed that pursuit of client choice and the assessment of needs should go hand in hand. In this chapter we will explore this proposition and consider the difficulties and dilemmas.

The notion of choice is closely bound up with quality of life criteria. A feature of the concept 'quality of life' is that it relates to issues which are important to everybody – clients included. We thus have a universal frame of reference within which to recognise what may be important issues of choice for individual clients in particular circumstances. For example, we would all recognise that quality of life includes access to choose from a range of different kinds of activities and places in daily living. We may therefore consider whether clients enjoy such choice and access, what kinds of different places they are able to reach, and whether access is denied to places where they would like to go.

This example illustrates a theme to which we shall keep returning: choice affects both major decisions – where to live, where to work, with whom to associate – and also detailed decisions about daily living: for example, what to wear, where to go, what to do. Assessment and care management link the big decisions and the smaller choices.

A further general point is that client participation in assessment, based on allowing maximum regard for expressed preferences, prepares the way for the client to be involved in care plans. It thereby helps to ensure linkage between assessment and care plans.

In Chapter Two we quoted the three quality of life groups of factors identified by Schalock:

- Environmental control
- Community involvement
- Social relations.

ENVIRONMENTAL CONTROL

None of us entirely controls our environment and many of us get frustrated that we cannot control it more. For example, many people feel frustrated about the issue of deciding whether the water we drink has fluoride added to it or not. But most of us do take for granted being able to decide about what to do in our own homes. Smoking and non-smoker's rights for example, provides another set of environmental issues.

We saw in Chapter One how good care practice is bound up with these day-to-day issues. Assessment and care management have to ensure that such good practice is adhered to. This is reflected in parts of the demonstration assessment Instrument described in Chapter Two.

Environmental control applies:

1. Within the house: choice of furniture, food, sleeping arrangements, when to get up and go to bed, whether to stay in or go out, when to receive visitors; also the opportunity to understand and feel part of the process of determining any necessary restrictions on the grounds of health, safety, or respect for the wishes and needs of others.

2. Outside the house: freedom to come and go, access to a suitable means of transport to pursue the range of regular or irregular activities desired – for example with regard to shopping, daytime activities, holidays and opportunities generally.

A major part of the assessment revolves around the extent of support or assistance needed and felt to be desirable to make these kinds of choices. It can be expensive in staff time. In one staffed house for people with learning disabilities, a whole afternoon had been spent in meetings between staff and residents to determine the colour and type of covers they should buy for the living room suite. But one could argue, 'How much time does a family spend considering a major purchase for the home?' It can be at least an afternoon! To offer less leads down the road to 'institutionalisation'.

COMMUNITY INVOLVEMENT

Choice here relates to the range of opportunities for activities with others in the community. It includes choices about work or retirement. Even in times of general unemployment, there can still be important choices – for example about part-time or voluntary work or other alternatives to employment. It includes choices about church attendance, leisure opportunities, political activities and so on. It includes choices about how to travel: walk, cycle, use public transport or be taken by private car.

All of these issues raise questions about the assistance and support clients will need to make choices and to act on them.

SOCIAL RELATIONS

We all expect the right to select our friends, opportunities to make new friends, and to be able to associate with as wide, or as narrow, a range of people as we would wish.

It is important to avoid assumptions about what people 'should' be doing or not doing in these ways. For example, most elderly people may prefer the company of other elderly people, but there are exceptions. Most single people prefer to have a room of their own, but there could be exceptions. Some people might opt for a more communal way of life.

The Demonstration Assessment Instrument (see Chapter Two) focused on relationship qualities. Here, again, the exercise of choice means that there will be no universally right range of qualities for everyone. Some people like to be cared for more than to care for others, others are happier with opportunities to do things, however limited, for other people. Some people like to be 'gate-keepers' to resources and like others to ask them for information. And so on. Choice in social relations means choice about roles and the opportunity to exercise these roles in ways which help fit in with others to develop a harmonious community.

Of course, relationships and roles do not always work for harmony – at least not without difficulties. Implementing choices entails support to overcome difficulties in social relations.

CHOICES FOR THE FUTURE

Assessment looks to the future. It is concerned with planning for the future with the client or group of clients. Here is where some of the apparently bigger decisions arise: where to live, who with; whether to change jobs; what new activities to take up. But the big decisions often depend on apparently relatively minor factors in the present situation – for example, convenience for a bus-route to reach work or being close (or sometimes not too close!) to a particular relative.

A PROFILE OF PREFERENCES

We suggest a consideration of choices for the groups of quality of life factors, together with choices about the future, should be combined to construct a *profile of preferences* for (i) individual clients and/or (ii) a group of clients sharing the same facilities.

Here is an example of an individual profile of preferences for one of the residents included in our research in a staffed house:

Profile of client preferences

Name of Client: Jenny

Environmental Control: Jenny wants a new bed-table, patterned wallpaper and 'my own phone by my bed'. Within the house, she wants the chance to do more sewing and 'would like to try using the hoover again'. She also wants more opportunities to go out.

Community Involvement: Her main interest in the community is to be with more friends, rather than in terms of activities or use of facilities.

Social Relations: She especially wants to be with more people of her own age – at the moment she is older than most of the others in the house.

Choices for the Future: Jenny would like to move to a smaller flat but in the same area in which she now lives, in order to be able to meet her friends easily and to use the same shops, etc. She wants to share the flat with someone her own age.

By putting the profiles of a group of clients together (in this case Jenny's co-residents) we can immediately see patterns:

(i) where preferences are congruent.

(ii) where preferences are not congruent.

Figure 12 shows an example of the summary of a profile of preferences for Jenny and some of the others in the staffed house where Jenny lived.

Extent of congruence

Four of the five residents in the group wanted more control over their lives – there is a theme of wanting more space, freedom and opportunity. Stuart is an exception: he wanted to feel more protected. This could make procedures for dealing with residents difficult in a group but it offers guidance for future planning.

Jenny wanted to mix and to live with people who were more of her own age-group. The project was able to arrange for her to live with a friend from outside the present house, so her wishes in this respect caused no care management complications.

Harold wanted to live with his girl-friend (another resident within the care of the same organisation) and this caused no difficulties on this account.

Several of the residents wanted to move; yet, for different reasons, they wanted to remain in the same area. This proved very difficult since there was a lack of suitable accommodation in that area. In this case what could be described as secondary choices have to be explored.

The question in this case would be: 'Would you rather stay where you are in order to be in this area, or move to another area?'. These are the kinds of choices we all have to make.

Stuart said he wanted to live with his 'boss'. This referred to his 'boss' for voluntary work he was doing at riding stables. This was a relatively rare example in our recent research of an expressed wish which was not realistic because the person concerned could not accommodate him. In this kind of situation, the secondary choice becomes: 'You cannot live with your 'boss' so where would you prefer to live instead?'

Client	Preferences regarding			
	Control of environment	*Community involvement*	*Social relations*	*Future*
Jenny	Bedside telephone; to do more things herself	To be with friends	With people her own age	Flat in same area with someone her own age
Harold	Room re-decorated; own TV; make own meals	To go out and about	To be with girl-friend	Live nearer grand-dad and to live with girl-friend
Cynthia	To go out occasionally without anyone or with someone different from usual. Less help shopping		To be with fewer people	Flat in the same area
Ben	Bigger wardrobe	Shopping by himself		Likes where he is
Stuart	Feels fright sometimes in his room and would like to change. Would like more help to do some things	Not enough help to go out		Would really like to live at his boss's house

Figure 12 Summary profile of preferences for a group of residents

It will be noted that one resident did not really want to move anywhere. This raises more complicated issues, which we discussed in Chapter Two. If the group preference is for moves away from a larger to a smaller facility or set of facilities, where does this leave a minority who may not want to move? This will lead to complex care management and service planning issues about the future use of the existing facility. The story in this particular case was very complicated indeed. Originally, the agency had decided to sell the house. In this case, Stuart would have had to move. Later, however, funding problems arose in connection with accommodating the residents whose support needs were the greatest and, in the event, the house was not sold so that these people (including Stuart) could stay on. But this decision, in turn, would have implications for the admission of future residents to take the places of the residents with less great support needs who were able to move. We shall be discussing the financial and management issues arising in this kind of situation in Chapter Six.

CLIENT PREFERENCES AND SUPPORT NEEDS

Having considered a profile of preferences, the next question is to relate it to the assessment of support needs. In other words, what are the support implications of fulfilling the expressed preferences of each client or of a group of clients? For example:

> Jenny wanted to live in a flat with a friend. She also *needed* to be on the ground-floor for health reasons. She *needed* a lot of support in a variety of ways and for various reasons. Her mobility was limited and she was diabetic. She needed some support in making meals and some assistance to board most public transport. Her key worker had commented that 'she does need a lot of care though this does not always appear to be so – therefore there is a risk.' The expressed wish to learn to hoover 'again' is interesting. Using a vacuum cleaner instead of cleaning with a carpet sweeper or brush would, generally, be associated with a better quality of life. Jenny wanted to be able (again) to be able to do this herself. Yet enabling her to do this, and coping with the risks of using an electrical appliance, might mean she would need *additional* rather than less support.

Jenny's wishes and support needs were managed by finding a flat which happened to be round the corner from a staffed house the agency was proposing to set up.

A general point to emerge from many of the examples considered so far is the right, and the need, of clients in staffed and supported accommodation to develop deep personal relationships. In exceptional cases, where people have been institutionalised most of their lives, this will include re-discovering close relationships with their parents or other family members. More generally, it will be with people outside their family – including loving relationships which may lead to lasting partnerships.

EXTENT OF CONGRUENCE BETWEEN CLIENT AND CARER WISHES

The assessment process is intended to take account of the views of the carer, and of others involved in the client's network of family and close friends. Often there is a congruence between these views and the preferences and needs of the client. Perhaps we too readily assume that this is the case. There can be conflicts.

Distinctions can be made between the following types of situations:

1. The carer and client disagree about what is best for the client. For example, a mother may feel she 'knows best' for her young son; or, perhaps, a son may feel he 'knows best' for his elderly mother.

2. The carer's own needs may conflict with the fulfilment of the wishes of the client. For example, an elderly person may wish to stay at home; the person at home looking after him or her cannot cope and 'needs' to have the chance to get away.

In the first kind of situation, the decision must rest with the client as to whether the carer's or his or her own views should prevail. The only exception would be on an objective judgement by the care manager that safety needs should prevail.

In the second kind of situation, there is no simple formula to guide us to the right answer, except to say that, in community care, the 'client' comprises sets of people in relationships with each other and not a single person in isolation. Here the normal social work skills and experience in harmonising family or other close relationships would apply.

In both types of situations, the assessment process is concerned with trying to talk through and to harmonise potential conflicts of interests, backed by support to make the agreed situation easier to cope with. This has resource implications for the ensuing care management (see Chapter Six).

We can sum up by saying that individual choice acquires meaning to the extent to which there is a range of options at different points in the assessment process: when the client first expresses preferences and, later, when these preferences are discussed in the light of the needs and preferences of others in the client's support network.

CLIENT CHOICE AND TYPES OF APPROACHES TO ASSESSMENT

The example we have used – namely Jenny and some of her fellow residents in a staffed house – was one where an assessment was based on an 'opportunities' approach (see Chapter Two). Our research demonstrated that, where assessment was based on this approach, client views were more likely to be taken into account in detail during the assessment and care management process than where other approaches to assessment prevailed.

PROBLEMS WITH A 'READINESS' APPROACH

At one project where a 'readiness' type of assessment was used, the care managers were inclined to recognise client choice along the single dimension of whether the residents wished to move towards more independence. The options were (i) to stay put (but, as in the earlier case, this was not really an option because it was planned to 'dispose' of the residents and use the facility for other purposes) (ii) to move to 'half-way' provision ('cottages') or (iii) to leave the area to be nearer to relatives.

Clients' views entered into the assessment in two respects. First, in a general sense, they reinforced the goal of the project – namely training for independent living. The assessments demonstrated that clients wanted this.

There is an element of absurdity here. You place people in a restrictive environment (a hostel), ask them what they want, and when they answer what amounts to saying 'fewer restrictions', this is used as evidence for alternative placements – which, however, they are not yet ready for because they have not been assessed in a freer 'half-way' house. You do not need a sophisticated assessment (and the assessments in this case were very sophisticated indeed, since assessment was the *raison d'etre* for the project) to reach these conclusions!

Second, in this case, the assessment did, for some clients, offer an option of moving to live nearer relatives. The option was rejected in two instances which we studied because the relatives said a move to somewhere closer to them would cause them to worry.

If relatives can be persuaded to take over responsibility, there is a let-out for a 'readiness for more independence' type of assessment – the responsibility is shifted back to carers.

Perhaps, in some instances, if this took place, clients would be swapping one type of restrictive environment (a hostel) for another. Their lives might now be restricted by parents – although, as stated earlier, we should not assume this. The 'readiness' approach to assessment did not evaluate the possibilities in these terms.

In other cases, client views counted insofar as they wanted moves to less restrictive placements; but they would have to wait until they, and suitable facilities, were 'ready' to fulfil their specific wishes. At the same time it was difficult for clients to exercise choices over a wide range of detailed aspects of daily living when their present environment was restricted. Hence the logical step of considering only a next step to a 'half-way' facility – this would be a place to give clients a taste of greater independence and at the same time the opportunity to make choices based on experiences they had not hitherto had.

PROBLEMS WITH A 'SUITABILITY' APPROACH

Options where there is a 'suitability' approach to assessment will depend on the range of provision available in any given instance. For example, in another project studied in the research, there was a choice of a number of single flats, double flats and a core house. Referrals were solicited through advertisement and, after a group had been chosen, there followed an allocation process.

Careful assessments had been undertaken by support workers for the prospective clients from a range of settings – hospital, staffed houses, flats, and for clients living with relatives. At the allocation meeting, each case was presented by the support worker concerned, while the project co-ordinator wrote on a flip-chart. He was particularly interested, after a general introduction, in the social support needs and adaptations that might be necessary. This was because the building work was currently in progress; in this respect, at least, the care management process could be described as needs-led. Yet, in the final process of allocation this was not the case. It was 'people for housing' and not 'housing for people'.

Part of the problem was that each support worker only had the detailed assessment knowledge of his or her particular client. They were in a weak position in a meeting conducted by a manager who, alone, had an overall knowledge. They were therefore reduced to bargaining, at least implicitly, on behalf of 'their' client in the allocation arrangements. As in the game of musical chairs, when the assessment, like the music, stops and action takes place, there is a rush to the most accessible vacant place. The clients were not there to share in the 'game'.

AN 'OPPORTUNITIES' APPROACH

The research found that, in contrast, where an opportunities approach to assessment prevailed, it was feasible to have more open-ended negotiations with others about the allocation of places. This was because the framework for the discussions ranged more widely than whether a particular facility, or even a set of facilities, was 'suitable'. Instead the questions were:

- How can we maximise concern for client choice based on every available opportunity?

- How can we maximise choice in different areas of the client's life, including living situation, work and leisure opportunities, enhancement of social network and so on?

- How can we be concerned about individual choices as well as about group choices?

We shall consider the more complex implications of fulfilling client wishes and needs in line with this approach in Chapter Five. First, however, we propose to look more closely at staff training issues in connection with assessment.

CHAPTER FOUR

Assessment Skills and Training Needs

Assessment has only recently come to be a topic in its own right in the field of placements and services for adults with learning disabilities. This was shown up during our research by the lack of evidence of assessments having taken place in the past when clients arrived from previous placements to their present placement.

While this may be less the case for other adult client groups, the practice in the past has often consisted of decision-making by individual professionals with little consultation with carers, relatives, or the client and with little in the way of recorded reasons for the placement decision.

TRAINING IN ASSESSMENT

A large proportion of residential and support staff today providing care in the community have no qualifications in the caring professions. The data from the research showed that, amongst officers-in-charge of hostels for adults with learning disabilities, nursing and social work qualifications were equally common. However, no residential staff claimed to have had any specific training in the assessment of people within the client-group(s) for whom they were responsible (in this case people with learning disabilities). Few had any knowledge of assessment instruments other than those they were actually using. Some had covered assessment in other areas of social work, for example on a pre-social work course at FE colleges.

It is to be hoped that the record of professional training, including training in assessment, will be better amongst care managers on the purchasing side. We have not yet any research to inform us about this. But assessment will involve both purchasers and service providers, since it is the providers who, especially in supported accommodation, will have the first-hand knowledge of the client on which the assessment will be based. Furthermore, the techniques we have recommended in Chapter Two, including client and staff diaries, will require informed active participation on the part of care and support staff. Good service providers will also want to be concerned with assessment routinely, as a continuous process, for the training they provide.

For all these reasons, we need to understand what the present difficulties are for staff in dealing with assessments.

FINDING TIME

There appeared from our research to be a great deal of difficulty in embracing assessment as an ongoing and vital component in giving good care to people with learning disabilities. In virtually every establishment it was reported that finding time to complete the assessment with clients in uninterrupted one-to-one interviews was almost impossible.

For Officers-in-Charge this raises the issue of organising staff in a special way to create such spaces without the staff feeling guilty about other necessary tasks being left to others. The current phrase used for finding time is 'prioritising', and that highlights the fact that the management have to give the message to staff that assessment is important enough to merit being given time alongside the more obvious daily tasks. There is, of course, a budgetary element also in creating such spaces, as extra hours may or indeed should be paid to workers whose schedule is already full to accommodate the assessment task.

In the words of one Development Officer: 'The thing is to get staff to see assessment as planning an individual's future, not a functional exercise.'

In the case of many residential settings in larger organisations, this would mean getting higher management to take account of this in planning staffing levels and conditions. In other words, there needs to be planning for assessment, to enable planning on the basis of an accurate picture of the needs of the client group.

To be involved in the assessment task is a daunting one for many residential workers who have no training or experience of it. The notes from our field research assistant show examples such as this:

One of the staff confided privately that he had felt quite inadequate to the task sometimes when he had been completing the Assessment Instrument. He clearly felt his lack of any professional training in a much stronger way than he had communicated during the staff meeting. What he said to me was that his lack of confidence about completing this task had actually affected his motivation to carry on with it.

Through participation in assessment, provided that they receive adequate training for it, staff can gain increased professional self-respect, interest in the job, recognition of progress (and also needs) in the residents in their care, and the understanding that they may be helping in an individual's development towards independence.

The first stage in the preparation of staff at any level to make assessments is for them to be convinced of the need for it.

THE PURPOSE OF THE ASSESSMENT

There are several circumstances which should occasion an assessment:

1. Moving on from Education Services. Those who have attended a Special School will have been the subject of a Record of Needs /Statement of Needs for the purpose of determining their special educational needs, and such a document relating to their strengths and needs as a adults will form the basis of their Future Needs Assessments.

   Clients regarded as having disabilities who have left school recently should be subject to the specific procedures laid down in the Tom Clarke Act (The Disabled Persons (Services, Consultation and Representation) Act (1986)).

   Staff should be aware of this legislation and of its implications for the continuation of assessment, including its implementation, from school to adulthood.

   An assessment of this type could be accomplished within a relatively leisurely time-scale, unlike many other occasions of assessment which relate to some impending event in the client's life.

2. Preparation for a move of home. Community care assessments often fall into this category, and workers need to understand the importance of a full picture of the client being produced in order to ensure that the move is the best one for them. Even if (deplorably!) the choice of provision may be no more than of the 'take it or leave it' type, a full assessment should help prevent inappropriate moves. Assessments can be undertaken at the request of the client or carer wishing a move.

3. Assessment for training. Specific training or teaching programmes may be on offer, particularly in day care settings; for example, practice in using public transport. The focus of assessment in this case would be specific, but could raise possibilities for wider assessments for clients not previously considered.

4. The review process. Clients who are receiving some services will have their whole situation reviewed at regular intervals. This is fairly widely established, for example in day centres, and ideally will have been broadened to include key workers, carers, and/or support workers from the client's home. The client and key relatives should be included. This process can be of great value in keeping all involved up-to-date with developments in the client and in the services he/she is receiving or making use of. The review meeting itself becomes an assessment of the client at that time.

   However, the potential benefits resulting from the review can be dissipated if significant workers are unable to attend, those entrusted with the execution of plans leave the post, or unrealistic recommendations are made at the review. The usefulness of the process hinges on careful assessments being made in advance by the workers involved, and written reports distributed prior to the meeting. Proper records should be kept of the discussion and, afterwards, a summary and agreed recommendations should be sent to those working with the client, in addition to the participants at the review.

WHO CARRIES OUT THE ASSESSMENT?

This will vary with the type of approach to assessment (see Chapter Two) but, assuming it is accepted that assessment is a process undertaken with the client, and not something done to the client, the assessment must be regarded as a collaborative exercise. To expect clients to make their own assessments without support or assistance from staff is as absurd as not to involve the client at all.

Nevertheless, it is possible for clients to complete some schedules, and answers recorded by another in the client's words are an invaluable part of an assessment which is centred on the individual client, his/her views and his/her choices.

The person with the most detailed knowledge of a client's abilities and limitations is the client. The people with the next most thorough knowledge of the client's skills and abilities are those, including family, who work with the client on a daily basis. This knowledge needs to be recorded in a form which can be understood by those who plan services in the broadest sense, in other words, from anyone who may have to do with the services that the client receives, to local and area managers and managers of organisations in the independent sector who may have responsibility for strategic planning as well as resource allocation for services for the group to which the client belongs.

An assessment instrument therefore requires to record the information about the client by asking questions of those who have the best knowledge. The assessment itself takes place when the person with the knowledge formulates an answer to the question. Thus we can have self-assessment, alongside assessment by carers, and (possibly less validly) assessment by professionals who do not know the client very well but who know what they are looking for in relatively brief encounters with the client. The importance of the distinction between producing the answer as a result of thinking about the question, and recording that answer is vital.

The person experienced in assessing clients in a particular group, and the person who knows the client well, may be able to convey a clear picture of the client and their needs without a list of questions. Indeed, our study produced some examples where workers preferred to write a series of concise, to-the-point paragraphs in their own style on an area of enquiry rather than stick to the format of the assessment instrument. However, in general it is the case that the quality of the design of the questions in an assessment instrument is critical in determining the usefulness of the results.

The ideal assessment instrument asks the questions in such a way as to enable those who lack professional training and self-confidence in assessment, and even the client, to produce information in a useful form.

The point has been made that the care manager or other person recording the data on the instrument does not require to know the client, provided the answers are coming from the client or others who do know the client well. However, in many cases the scenario is that the person completing the schedule does know the client well. This is a great help where the staff person can sensitively elicit what the client means despite communication difficulties or difficulties which the client may have in understanding the questions. Often they can remind the client of events and elaborate on the answer given. On the other hand, those who live or work closely with the client have their own views, for example about how easy or awkward the client is to get along with, and these attitudes can show through in responses to questions.

Where the schedules are completed not by support staff but by a care manager who does not know the client well, putting the questions to the client and the family members with whom the client lives, in our study the answers given by the family show an almost measurably deeper concern for their loved one, and the desire to give attention to every detail of their lives, capabilities and vulnerabilities. At the same time, there is the impression that the client's own voice may come through more faintly in the answers.

INFORMAL REVIEWS

We found this term being used to denote the discussions which go on between carers about clients. Usually it takes the form of a chat over coffee at the end of a shift or a discussion between parents talking over their concerns. In many ways it could be said that these are the occasions with the most potential for highlighting aspects of the client's strengths and limitations. Novice care workers find these to be the occasions where they learn most from those with more experience about their work and about assessment.

Unfortunately, the individuals involved in these discussions rarely feel they have any power to affect the outcomes for the clients they care for. Residential workers may feel (correctly) that any enhancements or services they might suggest for a client would be dismissed for lack of finance or because they lack the seniority to speak with authority on the procurement of resources. Parents, equally, although they have the best opportunity to find out what their sons or daughters need, are likely to feel helpless in the face of local authorities' statements that services are to be cut back, and may also, through isolation from other carers, have a very limited view of the possible options for their sons or daughters. For elderly clients the same will apply to the feelings of daughters (usually!) or other family members trying to care for their parents for as long as possible.

ASSESSMENT SKILLS

1. Motivation

Perhaps the most important qualification for a worker involved in an assessment is to see the value of doing the assessment, as outlined above. Unfortunately, many of the workers with responsibility for clients in our study did not have this perspective. Many were not sufficiently supported by their Officer-in-Charge, or were not given the necessary time during normal work schedules, or were not given the encouragement to believe that they and the client together had the knowledge to answer the questions. This led in some cases to somewhat perfunctory answers to the questions, and abandonment of the attempt at the more complicated parts, for example where a series of questions have to be repeated for different services received. The workers who were able to recognise the benefits in the more demanding aspects of the assessment process, for example daily diary recording, were more successful at keeping the clients going at it than colleagues who saw it as pointless.

Some workers felt that the assessment process had gone on interminably. All who raised this point agreed that to set deadlines for the completion of each section would have helped speed the process up, and perhaps provided added motivation to complete the task.

> *Skills needed: To sustain motivation.*

2. Data recording

Staff should recognise when fresh information needs to be gathered from the client or from other staff or other agencies, and when data which is already recorded can be used in completing a formal assessment schedule or questionnaire.

> *Skills needed: To distinguish when fresh data needs to be gathered, or existing data recorded.*

3. Observation

Although much of the information accrues over months and years, it is nevertheless extremely helpful for those doing the assessment to look at the questions some time before attempting to answer them. The period thereafter is when the assessments of abilities, potential, and limitations are being made. The questions previously read help staff to observe relevant events, reflect on them, and create opportunities to try out skills on the part of the client. This is equally true for self-assessment by the client and that done by a worker.

> *Skills required: Systematic observation, reflection and planning opportunities for further observation.*

4. Objectivity

People always have their own perspective on others, and particularly those they work with. It is important that workers completing an assessment instrument on behalf of a client are aware of their own feelings and attempt to record as helpful a picture as possible. Unhelpful examples from the research include the use of client's diaries as an opportunity to complain about the client being uncooperative about shaving himself, and again as a footnote to the diaries, a description of the number and variety of trips the establishment offered residents in the preceding month, along the lines of an advertisement. Some emphases in the recording on the other hand are justified, for example the fieldworker stating that they believed that the client would need much more support in a more independent living situation in keeping her room clean and tidy, despite the fact that she was perfectly competent at this in the present living situation.

> *Skills needed: Self-insight to make objective judgements on another's needs.*

5. Reading, writing, and thinking ability

The assessment Instrument was completed in writing by two clients themselves. This would not be possible for the majority and, even where clients can record their own assessment, the exercise is still one that should be shared. It is also to be hoped that an experienced, caring, thoughtful worker would be able to use the questions and the process of answering them more fully in order to convey an accurate, detailed, and useful account of the client's abilities.

Some workers found difficulty with the Instrument, describing it as 'too academic', and one Deputy Officer-in-Charge proposed to have as little as possible to do with it because she 'didn't like paperwork'. In this context, part of the problem for some residential workers was lack of confidence in their own literacy skills. While this need not affect in any way their ability as care staff, it would appear that in-service training on report-writing and similar skills would be of considerable value.

> *Skills needed: Reading, writing and clear thinking.*

6. Seeing things from the stance of an outsider who will be using the assessment

Some staff in completing the assessment instrument may fail to grasp that those wishing to draw information from the document will not know anything about the client other than what was included there. An example from the research will illustrate the problem: did the entry 'goes out with sister' mean that the client went out socially with a relative, or was she taken out by a member of staff who happened to belong to a religious order? The latter turned out to be the case. Such diary entries can be significant if there are no other references to family contact, and the client is stated to be unable to cope with going out except when escorted. Another example is of a client's place of residence being given as 'Lilac Grove'. Careful piecing together of other clues led to the conclusion that the client lived independently, possibly with a flatmate or neighbour with learning disabilities (mentioned in diary as 'shares Lilac Grove'). However, only further enquiries of someone who lived locally revealed that Lilac Grove is a sheltered housing complex.

In some cases, the assessment is for an already-existing provision. In that case the assessment can be given helpful emphasis to clarify questions relevant to the prospective placement. However, this can be carried to extremes, as in the case of the young woman in a long-stay hospital who was being assessed for placement in a supported flat in the community. Virtually all of the diary entries for that client were about shopping, cooking, and washing up, and how well or otherwise she did it, as though that was the only aspect of her life or activities that was relevant to the assessment.

> *Skills needed: To record in ways that will make sense to the reader who does not necessarily know anything about the client.*

7. Finding out what clients really think

The ability to listen well is a skill which care workers need to develop. It can be particularly difficult to avoid imposing one's own view when the client has difficulty in expressing what they feel. The communication problems of the clients in our research ranged from having only six words and using pointing to indicate desires to having a memory so poor that no names could be used accurately. In the most severe of these cases, it was not possible to record the client's views in a very complex form, but it was still possible for the answers to show sensitivity, patience and understanding on questions of the client's views. Skill and sensitivity are certainly required to provide the guidance to enable the client to give a meaningful and true answer, without prompting the client to give back the answer thought of by the worker.

One important aspect of this is to explain the choices which are open to the client. It is difficult for the client to imagine the alternatives when posed the question 'Would you like to stay where you live now?' One excellent suggestion which came from one of the workers was to show the clients a video, depicting the alternatives which might be available to them.

> *Skills needed: To understand what clients wish to communicate about their preferences.*

8. Making sense of the client's answers

A place may be provided on the assessment document for recording disagreements between client and worker on the answers. Some workers raised the issue of whether to record what the client actually said or what the worker inferred from their remarks. This can be an area of difficulty, especially if a worker does not wish to undermine a client by demonstrating how unrealistic the answers that have been given are. On the other hand, to slavishly record misleading information because the client has said it is clearly doing the client a disservice, as it is likely to lead to an inaccurate assessment. In such cases the worker must have the confidence to append a qualifying note giving his/her own view of the situation.

It can also be necessary for workers to cross-reference answers from one part of the assessment instrument to another, because apparent inconsistencies arise. This can be partly due to the different parts of the assessment instrument being completed after gaps of some weeks. It actually provides a helpful check on the seriousness of the answers to be able to ask a question on a related area on a different occasion.

> *Skills needed: To interpret what clients are communicating, to look for patterns of consistency.*

9. Motivating the client to participate

While some clients are glad to participate, and may enjoy the experience of doing the assessment and diaries, others will be reluctant. A very useful skill in such a situation is to be able to convey to the client the way in which an assessment could benefit them. Of course to raise expectations of change when there are no resources to back them is, in the long run, not only cruel but counter-productive. Also, for some clients, especially elderly ones who are quite content in their living situation, the suggestion of positive changes would fall on deaf ears. One Officer-in-Charge commented on the process of participating in the assessment as having been stressful for some of his residents, as it had raised the unresolved issue of the future existence of their home. Being asked questions about their preferences in living situation and so forth, not surprisingly gave rise to their suspicion that some unwelcome changes were afoot.

> *Skills needed: Motivating the client to participate, not always in easy circumstances.*

10. Computer Literacy

For some existing assessment instruments on the market, and as further assessment instruments are developed, the recording of the assessment will be possible direct onto computer. Children who are being educated now, including children with learning disabilities, have no fear of using computers in everyday life.

At least one of the clients in our study, a blind man with mild learning disability, uses a small word-processor diary. Staff at one hostel where a computer version of the assessment instrument was piloted were said to be alarmed at the prospect, having never been near a keyboard before. This difficulty could be easily overcome by an in-service course to demystify the computer and teach basic keyboard skills.

> *Skills needed: The ability to use a computer and make others feel confident about using one.*

11. Liaison with other agencies

The ability to communicate with staff in other settings could be expected in care workers who take their job seriously. The problem is that, for many, the opportunity to put this into practice does not often arise. The nature of caring work is that it is seldom mobile. While care managers and the clients themselves travel around and may meet and do quite a lot with many different people, the care workers are much less likely ever to be in the company of workers in a different establishment. The assessments showed a considerable lack of knowledge on the part of care staff about what went on in the parts of the client's life when they were away. Clients' diaries, unless completed simultaneously in the home and day centre, contained empty spaces when the client was somewhere else. This is clearly a barrier to meeting the needs of clients in a coherent way, and is especially significant when the nature of the client's problem means that the he or she cannot keep track of complex systems and organisation.

This was well demonstrated in the assessment of one client which was recorded by the research fieldworker (who had no prior knowledge of the client being assessed):

> She completed the questions in consultation with the client himself, who has a speech defect and is difficult to make out. Although the information recorded was fairly accurate, when checked with the client's hostel keyworker, there were significant omissions and confusions. In addition when the information acquired from the hostel keyworker was checked with the day centre, and a voluntary group he attended, further misapprehensions on the part of the hostel staff came to light. They were mistaken about which college the client attended for what courses, whether he was receiving speech therapy, and who paid for his holiday the previous year. There was also a difference of view on the future plan for the client and how he was to be prepared for a move.

Skills required: To be able to find out about the client's life in other contexts accurately and coherently.

---

12. Adopting unaccustomed roles

One field social worker who completed the assessment instrument tried at first to do so without writing the answers down at the time, filling them in later from memory. She had to abandon the attempt because of the difficulty of carrying the amount of information all at once. This exposed the problem which social workers, by training and habit, have with writing during an interview with a client. However, for the purposes of assessment it is vital to keep an accurate record of what the client says. In fact, it should be interpreted as affording the client respect to be directly recording what he/she says for the purpose of passing it on accurately to decision-makers and those who may be allocating resources.

A problem area for care workers was the completion of sections of the assessment which attempt to calculate the cost of care. These sections are not intended to be completed without the client's knowledge. However, care staff felt that to draw attention to the fact that they are paid workers might change the client's view of them as confidant and friend into that of someone simply doing a job. In fact, it seems unlikely that a worker who is friendly, trusted and confided in would lose that earned relationship through the acknowledgement of the truth that he/she is an employee.

Calculation of the costs of a proposed care plan for any one client may also entail liaison with other agencies. Staff other than Officers-in-Charge found it virtually impossible to obtain the information about salaries and other costs in both their own place of work and other services used by the client. Any inclusion of costs in an assessment for services requires training for staff in overcoming inhibitions in this area, as well as more openness on the part of service providers about the costs of the services.

In many cases it is easier for care managers to approach other agencies about costs.

> *Skills needed: To be prepared to extend one's roles to participate fully in assessment and care management.*

TRAINING

Training for assessment should recognise that professional skills, knowledge and judgements are required. All staff involved should receive training. Care staff, most of whom lack formal qualifications, are in the front line for gathering information on which assessments are based, and training is especially important for them. Care management staff and senior staff on the service provision side too, though they are more likely to have a professional qualification, may lack the training and experience of holistic assessments for care management that are required.

We hope this book provides a text for such training.

CHAPTER FIVE

From Assessment to Placement Packages

'Placement packages' or 'packages of care' are jargon terms used in the community care literature to convey the idea that, following a comprehensive (or 'holistic') needs-led assessment, the various plans different agencies and informal carers have for meeting a client's needs are brought together to form a coherent whole. An example is suggested below in the case of a client called Janet. Janet is elderly and lives in a single flat in sheltered housing.

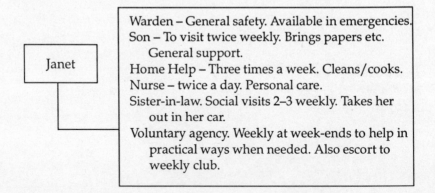

Janet

Warden – General safety. Available in emergencies.
Son – To visit twice weekly. Brings papers etc.
    General support.
Home Help – Three times a week. Cleans/cooks.
Nurse – twice a day. Personal care.
Sister-in-law. Social visits 2–3 weekly. Takes her
    out in her car.
Voluntary agency. Weekly at week-ends to help in
    practical ways when needed. Also escort to
    weekly club.

Figure 13 A package of care for Janet

The assumptions in putting together and operating such a 'package' are:

> • The people and services mentioned are aware of the part they play in relation to the parts played by others.

- The plan has been arrived at through agreement between those concerned and the client (Janet).

- As a result of the services provided, the client (Janet) will have greater opportunities to enjoy a better quality of life in keeping with her own wishes.

The results of operating such a package are referred to as 'outcomes'. The services provided are referred to as service 'inputs'. In Janet's case, the assessment and planning began when she was living alone in a large house by herself after her husband had died. In such cases, where a change of accommodation was included in the package of care, we also refer to the outcome as a 'placement outcome'.

In some cases, it may be that, following an assessment, it is decided that the client remains in her present house. This can still be referred to as a placement outcome if, amongst the options being considered, a possible move featured.

Thinking of care packages in terms of service inputs and placement outcomes provides a framework for evaluating the process of assessment and care management. It enables us to say that better placement outcomes are associated with certain features of the planning and care management process and that other features are detrimental.

Amongst the features our research considered are the following:

- Whether the assessment and care packaging process was continuous or whether it featured breaks due to extraneous factors or circumstances.

- Whether the care planning arose in the context of planning for a group of clients, or if the client's package of care was determined without direct reference to other clients.

- Whether the assessment and care planning arose only because of some outside event – for example, the closing of a hospital ward.

- The type of approach to assessment and care management, including breadth, flexibility and specificity.

We will examine each of these sets of issues in turn.

CONTINUITY FROM ASSESSMENT TO CARE MANAGEMENT

Continuity from assessment to care management was found in our research often to be hindered by two related kinds of fragmentation. First, what are often called 'programme assessments' were seen as entirely separate from future living assessments.

A 'programme assessment' means an assessment of service goals and the client's progress towards meeting these goals. For example, clients' training programmes may be assessed using various scales, for example Copewell scales. These scales, measuring a client's performance will have implications for future living assessments. Yet the two assessment processes are sometimes kept separate. In one area included in our research the placement decision was reached without reference to programme assessments.

Second, different agencies, or perhaps different sections within the same agency, had piecemeal assessment responsibilities. In the example just quoted, the placement decision followed a review attended by various professionals each of whom had, furthermore, made their own assessments.

The ensuing negotiation between professionals gathered in this way to make decisions based on fragmented assessments tended to follow a narrow consideration of (i) whether the client was ready to move from the present placement or should stay put and (ii) whether he or she was suitable for a specified alternative placement where there was thought to be a vacancy.

The research found that these problems were more likely to be overcome if both the present placement situation and possible alternative placements were controlled by the same agency. On the other hand, even where different agencies were involved, a flexible approach based on an overall care management control could bring about the desired kind of careful needs-led planning.

The care manager must have sufficient authority to achieve such control and collaboration. Assessment for care management means the gathering of relevant information from different sources to make a single assessment, undivided by separate disciplines, professional groupings or agency ideologies. Care management means carrying the assessment process through as possibilities (options) are considered with the client, and with the agencies and other sources of support concerned.

The independence of the purchaser from the service provider (or potential service provider) should make it easier to cross boundaries. Tact and negotiating skills are important.

For example, to go back to the question of the separation between a programme assessment and a holistic assessment for a care plan, obviously the former should help to inform the latter. The care manager must recognise that he or she depends on the detailed knowledge of the client's needs from the various existing service providers. Programme assessments are necessary. It is a mistake either:

1. To ignore available assessments and service plans from individual services. The best approach is to suggest that the service provider is likely to know much about the client that is necessary to formulate a care plan.

2. To think that a range of assessments from individual services can take the place of a holistic care plan.

Even if an existing service (for example a day service) claims to have a 'holistic plan' for a client embracing a range of different aspects such as work, leisure, survival skills, and so on, it will still be open to bias as a service-led assessment. The care manager is in the more detached position as purchaser to ensure that such an assessment is holistic and needs-led. For example:

> Bill had followed an intensive 12-month life-skills programme in a special project. As a result, detailed assessment material was available about his self-care and daily living strengths and weaknesses, as well as more limited information about some of his preferences for the future. It was known, for example, that he wanted to live with his girl-friend. However, the agency responsible for Bill's life-skills programme knew very little about the needs of the girl-friend.

Traditionally, as we said earlier, such different perspectives might be brought together at a case conference, review or resources allocation meeting of some kind. The differences between this and care management are shown in Figure 14. The traditional approach entails bargaining been different agents who have partial knowledge of the client's total situation and future needs. It also tends to be focussed on a group decision at a single meeting. Care management, on the other hand, combines – as the name suggests – (i) a process (based on client care) of moving from the implications of a coherent, whole assessment (which may be informed by separate partial assessments) to planning and (ii) personal management. Community care is the product of personal management involving negotiations with service providers and potential providers, rather than the product of group consensus.

It will also be seen from Figure 14 that, with the traditional process, resource allocation tends to follow after a placement decision has been taken. Our research was especially concerned with the lack of linkage at this point. In contrast, the role of the care manager incorporates both placement decision and resource allocation. We shall be looking at this aspect of care management in later chapters.

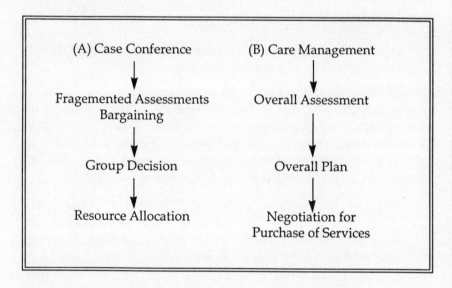

Figure 14 A comparison between placement decision-making (A) by traditional case conference and (B) by care management

INDIVIDUALISED OR BATCH PROCESS

Care management is based broadly on the principle of individualisation. This is one of the oldest principles in social work – the original meaning of 'case work' means working on an individual 'case by case' basis instead of dealing with 'batches' of people in a standard way. The care in the community legislation assumes that clients are assessed individually and that care plans will be made to meet their needs on an individual basis. At the same time, there is a much broader focus than there might have been in traditional casework.

Our research found, however, that for many people in supported accommodation, plans were being made for groups of people rather than for individuals. This could be for various reasons. Perhaps a decision had been taken to close a hostel and to transfer the residents to smaller homes. Perhaps a new home or cluster of flats was being opened and groups of clients were being sought to fill the vacancies. Perhaps, because of a new policy or new management (or both) all client placements in a given area or facility were being simultaneously reviewed. Whatever the reason, planning decisions about clients in supported accommodation especially have often been taken in terms of groups of clients rather than individually. We decided in our research to refer to this phenomenon as 'batch' processing.

The following examples make the distinction between individual and batch assessment and care management clearer.

An example of batch processing

Adler's Home had been designated a special assessment project. The Home was to be closed and all the residents were to be assessed to see to what extent they could be progressed to independent living. As a result, some moved to flats, some to 'half-way houses' and one resident with dementia was expected to be admitted to hospital.

In this case, while each client had an individual assessment, the planning process was conceived and implemented in terms of all of the residents as a group. They were to be dispersed from a fairly large home to other supported accommodation in smaller groups.

An example of individual processing

Mr Smith was a long-term resident in a psychiatric ward of a small general hospital. He was attending a day service in the community. The staff at the day centre, during the course of a routine assessment, wondered in view of the progress Mr Smith had made and because of his dislike of hospital, whether suitable accommodation could not be found for him in the community. This set in motion a holistic assessment of his needs for future living in keeping with care in the community.

Mr Smith is an interesting case because we might generally associ-ate moves from hospitals to the community with batch processing – with a decision, for example, to close a hospital ward (or a whole hospital). But Mr Smith's assessment arose solely because of an initiative on the part of his day service key worker to respond to his particular needs and wishes, independently of plans for any of the other clients.

The distinction, then, between individual and batch processing can be summed up by saying that the former occurs independently from the plans of other clients in the same situation. Batch process-ing occurs where plans for a group of clients are being considered together, and where the moves of one client may well affect others.

In particular, in a batch situation, such as the one described above as Adler's Home, the question arises, what should happen where there is a conflict between the declared policy for the group of clients as a batch and the individual needs of different clients? What happens if, after the assessment, it is seen that some of the clients should really not be moving at all but should stay where they are, but a decision has been taken to close the home, or to change its use?

One answer is to view such policy decisions, like a decision to close down a home, as inevitable facts of life and to operate a needs-led care management as far as possible within these limits. After all, it might be argued, we are all subject to some constraints because of the decisions of planners and others. Our house might be subject to a compulsory purchase order, or we might have to move because we can no longer afford to pay the rent or the mortgage.

Policy, however, affecting placements should itself be under the most careful scrutiny as a part of care management. Care manage-ment, policy and planning should be closely inter-related. All of these should be based on the standards of good practice discussed in Chapter One. For example, we know that a sense of security is especially important for the vulnerable clients who will be subject to care management. That they should be subject to forced moves because accommodation is shut down, unless it is clearly unsuit-able, or is contrary to providing a sense of security.

Much depends on how batch moves are handled; to what extent, when and how clients are informed and involved in the decisions. The research produced some contrasting examples of practice in this respect.

The clients of one home, St Hilda's, felt very insecure because they were subject to rumours about the home's future which kept changing. First the home, run by a voluntary organisation, was going to be taken over by the local authority. Then, it seemed, this proposal was scrapped and it was to be sold off to another agency. Clients did not know whether they were to be allowed to stay on, whether they would all have to move, or how much say they would have in the decisions affecting their future. They were not systematically informed, let alone consulted.

In contrast, we have the case of Gladys (see Chapter Two):

After an individualised assessment based on an opportunities approach, a package of care was carefully planned with her and with her participation in discussions about placement possibilities. There were to be disappointments. The first flat she hoped to get turned out not to be available. Of course she was disappointed, but her insecurity was managed by keeping her fully involved, as well as fully informed, about what was going on. She knew precisely what option was being considered, with whom, what the problems were, why there was a disappointment and what alternative possibilities there would be.

The differences in these two examples are highlighted below:

St Hilda's	Gladys
* Decisions about the future taken away from the clients	* Care plans determined by Gladys's assessment
* Clients not kept informed on a regular basis	* Gladys kept informed on a regular basis
* No policy for dealing with clients' feelings of insecurity	* Gladys's feelings of insecurity carefully managed

Figure 15 Contrasting examples of practice in batch moves

An unexpected finding from the research was that batch processing was, after all, as likely to be associated with good placement outcomes for clients as individualised processing. This was because batch situations tended to be where clients were leaving larger staffed units to find smaller units where they would enjoy greater independence. For clients who could manage such independence, placement finding was relatively straightforward. There were much greater problems in accommodating clients who needed to move to smaller staffed units (see Chapter Six). Individualised placement processes, on the other hand, included more complex situations – it was because they were complex situations that they had been singled out as priority cases for care management, and it was because solutions were harder to find that outcomes were no better than the outcomes from batch situations.

EVENT-DETERMINED ASSESSMENTS AND CARE MANAGEMENT

By 'event-determined' we mean the kind of situations we have referred to which are associated with batch processing – units forced to close down, changes of ownership or management, and so on. However, batch processing is not the only possible response to such events. The conditions for individualised processing include:

- sufficient time and effective time management
- sufficient control over associated events

Gladys' case is a good example of a situation where an event-determined assessment was shown to be compatible with an individualised care management process. The home where she was living was, as a matter of policy, being closed down. But the closure was planned to allow ample time for a range of alternative options to be considered for each resident.

Control over associated events meant that, in Gladys' case, although she had no control over the fact that her present home was being closed, she and her care manager did have some control over what was happening in connection with the alternatives, as well as with the care management process itself – who was involved, what facilities could be considered, what approaches were being made and so on.

To summarise, then, we can say that care management must, in some cases, be undertaken in response to events relating to the provision of services (as well as, of course, in response to events in the clients' own lives). However, event-determined care management does not need to entail a batch processing. An individualised approach to care management is still feasible, provided there is effective time management and control.

BREADTH, FLEXIBILITY AND SPECIFICITY

Care packaging is essentially about detail – the detail that will follow the detailed findings from the assessment about the client's lifestyle, current services and daily living needs and growth-potential. The research found that good placement outcomes were associated with care packaging perspectives that were broad, flexible and specific in terms of the detail.

A social network approach is especially useful for monitoring these perspectives. We ask:

- What are the people, places and activities that are important in the client's present living situation?

- If it is proposed to change this living situation, how will the social network be affected – for example, access to the people, places and activities that are important?

Two further concepts are useful. The first is the idea of identifying 'growth points' with reference to an enhanced quality of life. Granted that the client is in a particular situation, with reference to support received in daily living and in the light of possible opportunities, one asks 'what next?' What is the next step? And what are the resource implications?

The second idea, related to the first, is the notion of placement 'enhancement'. Whatever placement option is chosen, it is not simply a place of residence. The situation is open to selecting further options – for example a particular room, or particular decisions about independence – and to additional provision. For example, special additional arrangements can be considered to further the client's particular needs or interests. We refer to all these things as 'enhancements'.

We are suspicious of service plans or other statements about packages of care which are very brief – however elaborate the assessment on which they are based. For example: 'move to... (placement) where... (client) will have greater opportunities'. One needs to know:

- what opportunities?
- where?
- provided by whom?
- with what support?
- transport implications

And one needs to know these details in relation to:

- work (or education)
- leisure activities and special interests
- access to normal community facilities
- access to specialist facilities and services
- access to informal support
- special relationships – family and peer-group

The key question is how care plans will affect each of these aspects of daily living. Has the package of care taken them all into account, or was one major decision taken – about accommodation or about some other major service or facility – with the hope that the other aspects of the client's life would, somehow, fall into place? In our own personal planning, many of us find that it is the detailed considerations that often affect the major decisions – about buying a house, for example. We do not (do we?) buy a house on the basis of one or two major criteria – perhaps its size and price, important as these are. We look at all sorts of detailed issues: which way it faces, the number of windows and how these affect the light, features of the neighbourhood, convenience for the shops, the church or whatever, and so on. Care packaging should be about just these kinds of detail as well as about major determining factors.

There are advantages in using a network approach to display and record such detail. Figure 16 shows the social network for a client called Miss Benton who, at the time of her assessment, was living in a large house called Shirewood with 16 other residents. As a result of the assessment, it was decided that she had progressed sufficiently in learning to look after herself to be accommodated in a supported flat run by a housing association.

The diagrammatic display immediately highlights the extent of Miss Benton's involvement with a large network of relations, notwithstanding that she herself lived in a residential home. It was vital that, in any care package negotiated with the housing associa-

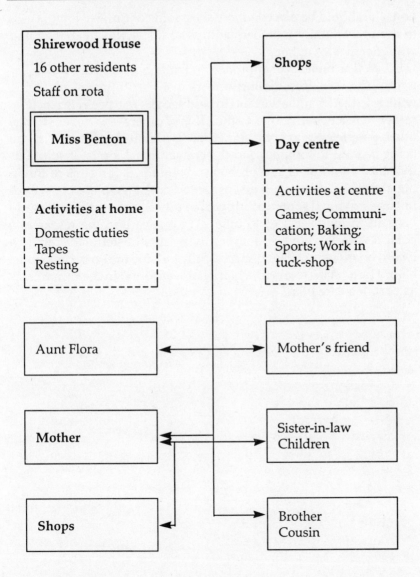

Figure 16 Network diagram showing implications of an assessment for care packaging

tion, she should be placed where she could continue to have access to the other family members with whom she was in contact and who meant a lot to her.

As well as breadth of approach and attention to detail, flexibility is important in formulating care plans. Flexibility means being willing to use imagination and to be able to have a positive reaction, rather than a negative one, to the ideas of others – however strange other people's ideas may sometimes seem at first! It may mean being willing to look beyond the conventional kinds of solutions for placement issues and problems. Sometimes it means re-thinking about the client – not just as the potential recipient of services but as a potential source of support to others, or as a person able to be paid to give services to others. In one case in the research, a person with learning disabilities living in a hostel managed by a health board was working successfully outside the hostel as a home help. The job was retained when a flat was found in the community as part of a care plan.

CHAPTER SIX

Costing and Resource Targeting

Front line social workers often resist the idea of being involved in costing services. Yet they alone have the information about the services provided to clients, and the client's use of these services, on which effective costing can be based.

The assessment Instrument used in our research incorporates procedures for estimating costs. Yet when we have been asked by a variety of agencies to make use of this Instrument, we are often told that they will not be using the bits of the assessment concerned with costing! Costing is seen to be a separate administrative exercise, carried out 'somewhere else'.

We suggest that costing services can, and should, be carried out at the same time as assessments. This may also help to demystify costing so that social workers and their clients can understand it.

As recently as 1989, research we carried out into the costs of supported accommodation throughout Scotland revealed that local authorities were not in a position to give an accurate picture of the costs of their residential or related services for an individual client. Some authorities could do rather better with their day services. A few authorities combined residential and day services, for costing purposes, in a way which made it impossible for them to separate the costs out.

When we returned to research costs in 1991–2, we found the position was changing in preparation for the new community care legislation. Most agencies could now give reasonable estimates of 'unit costs' for their services.

'Unit costs' means the costs of a given service divided by the number of clients using that service. Private agencies can very readily provide information about costs in these terms. Statutory service providers, since April 1993, should also be able to do this. But how useful are 'unit costs'? As a basis for charging fees they are a convenience. They can also be misleading. Our research showed that they can be dangerously misleading when it comes to the question of costing alternative placements for the purposes of needs-led service development.

The alternative to a unit-costs approach is one based on what we call 'real costs'. This means the costs of the actual usage of a service by a given client. This can be estimated by adjusting some of the components (variable costs) in the unit cost with regard to indicators of usage – the most important of these being the extent of the demands on staff time. Thus, in the case of a residential home, for example, 'real costs' comprise:

1. A fixed proportion of costs, which are generally very similar for all residents: for example rent, heat, light, administration and other overheads. (For some clients, heat might not be seen as 'fixed'.)

2. A variable proportion of unit costs where there are major differences between clients – for example use of care or support staff, transport. Food might be a variable cost if there are different arrangements for some clients – for example some clients buying their own food and cooking it themselves while others receive meals.

As the caveats in the above definitions suggest, the distinctions between fixed and variable costs will vary in different circumstances. A 'real costs' approach is concerned just with these *individual* differences.

'Real costs' can never be estimated as accurately as unit costs. This is not important, however. If we can estimate 'real costs' to the nearest £500 of annual revenue expenditure, it will be a far more useful indicator of costs for the purposes of needs-led care management than being able to estimate unit costs to the nearest penny, *because unit costs will give a misleading picture of the support costs for that client, in real terms.*

Let us consider, for example, the costs in relation to ten clients living in a hostel. (What follows is a real example taken from the research, which had major implications for resource targeting) (Seed, 1993):

> The total revenue expenditure for the year under review at this hostel was £143,000. Since there were ten clients, the unit (revenue) costs can be expressed as £14,300. This figure was used as the basis for a fee charged to the purchaser.

However, the agency providing the service estimated that only £14,100 of the total project expenditure was attributable to the costs of two of the ten clients. These two were not actually living in the hostel. They lived in a nearby flat, but, for administrative purposes, were regarded as being part of the hostel population since they were supported by staff from the hostel. If this sum of £14,100 is subtracted from the total cost of £143,000, it leaves £128,900 to be divided between the remaining eight clients – raising the unit cost for these eight to £16,100. (The unit cost for the two in the flat, taken separately, is reduced to £7,050 – less than half the cost for those resident in the hostel.)

The support and other variable costs for the eight clients living in the hostel were studied in our research. We found that, for two of them, who were living in a separate flat within the hostel, the real costs were about £12,000. (It was adequate, as we have said, to estimate to the nearest £500.) This finding meant that the unit costs for the remaining six would now work out at about £18,000. In fact, we estimated that real costs for these six varied between £16,000 and £21,000.

Thus, while the original unit cost for the ten clients was quoted by the agency to be £14,300, real costs for these clients varied from about £7,000 to three times this amount, namely £21,000. The purchaser was paying the same amount in each case.

These differences had major implications when we came to consider prospective placement moves from the hostel to smaller units in the community, in keeping with the policy of the agency.

The service plan was to move four of the clients with the highest support needs to a staffed house. The budget estimate (revenue) for this was £109,000 (excluding 'start-up' costs). This amounted to an estimated unit cost of £27,000. The agency told us that the staffing costs for a house of four residents would not be much less than staffing a house for eight. But it was their policy to keep the number at four, consistent with the high quality service they were in business to provide. A house for four, not eight, was also consistent with the findings of the needs-led assessment based on an opportunities approach.

Thus, on a unit cost basis, the agency was faced with increasing its charges for these four clients from the £14,300 charged for them at the hostel to the projected £27,000 in the new accommodation. They were told by the purchaser that this expense was unacceptable. The moves were postponed.

However, had charges been based on a 'real costs' basis from the start, the projected increases would have been much less dramatic. For the client whose costs were greatest, it would have been from £21,000 to £27,000 – still a substantial increase of £6,000, but not the 100 per cent increase that appeared on a unit costs basis, and which was rejected.

> In contrast, the 'real costs' for the clients with lower support needs who left the hostel were reduced when alternative supported but unstaffed flats were offered – and these reduced costs were, of course, readily accepted by the purchaser. The result was that plans were made for those with lower support needs to move, while those with higher support needs were left behind. This, in turn, raised questions about filling the places vacated by the first group, since the agency could not afford this level of 'voids' (unfilled places).

In other words, in the larger staffed hostel situation, the residents with less support needs were subsidising the costs of the clients with greater support needs. When both groups were expected to leave the hostel for smaller living units, the subsidy was removed.

We found in the research that situations like this were common, although the case quoted was, perhaps, an extreme example.

To understand the situation more clearly, we devised what we called a 'continuum of specificity' for services and costs. Figure 17 shows a Table for this continuum, showing clients' levels of support needs and expected levels of costs.

A hostel (by which we mean a staffed house for eight or more residents), is least specific in terms of unit costing of its services. In other words, here there are likely to be the greatest variations between the unit costs and the real costs for individual clients. The smaller staffed house is likely to be more specific, because the clients selected for living there are likely to require fairly similar levels of support. (This does not have to be the case, but it would need to be a very well thought-through care plan to justify combining a small number of clients with very different levels of support together, using the resources required for full staffing.)

The unstaffed house is likely to be the most specific of all for costing purposes. Here the gap between unit and real costs will be minimal. (If there is only a single client, of course, the unit cost *is* the real cost.) In an unstaffed house or flat, support (supplied off-site) is task-specific and time-specific. Staff are not simply 'there', on duty, as they are in a staffed situation. They are only employed (and therefore only costed) to come and go for particular client support purposes at particular times.

It follows that an unstaffed house is likely to be the most cost effective placement in real terms (for suitable clients). Not only are

Accommodation	Specificity	Numbers	Support needs	Costs
1. Hostel	Low	Large	Varied	Lower
2. Staffed house	Medium	Smaller	High	High
3. Un-staffed house	High	Small	Lower	Low

Figure 17 Continuum of specificity for types of supported placements

the overall costs less, (e.g. overheads) but the service is more specifically tailored to meet individual need. This is consistent with good practice in care packaging, which emphasises high specificity in looking at prospective placements (see Chapter Five).

This does *not* mean that unstaffed but supported accommodation is *always* cheap. It is possible to provide intensive off-site support for clients with high levels of support needs – and this, will, of course, be expensive. But whether it is cheap or expensive, the costs will reflect the specific needs of the clients and not the costs of sustaining a residential regime.

Figure 17 shows that the highest costs occur at the middle point in the specificity continuum. This would apply to the proposed staffed house for the four clients discussed earlier. Staff are employed to undertake support tasks which are likely to be more specific to the needs of individual clients than in a larger hostel, but less specific than in the case of an unstaffed house. They are still likely to have duty shifts providing continuous cover and with overlapping shifts at periods of peak demand. This, of course, is what makes them so expensive.

The question arises as to at what point, in meeting client needs, accommodation has to be staffed. The question of 24-hour cover may not be the main issue since modern technology can facilitate an effective emergency response. The main question is whether a client needs continuous supervision or other forms of staff attention during waking hours. This must apply to people with profound and certain kinds of multiple disabilities. It will also apply to people who are physically fit but who have major problems in controlling their behaviour, or in understanding their environment, and who therefore are a perpetual danger to themselves and/or others. For these people there must be the jump from the third to the second point on the continuum and hence a major jump in costs. In other words, they do need constant attention – but they do not need to be in hostels!

It is possible to consider 24-hour cover in unstaffed accommodation, where the level of demand for staff attention will not be so heavy in terms of *continuous* attention but where emergencies could arise at any time. As we have said, the functions of the staff will be time-specific and task-specific. Provided these conditions can be met, consistent with the opportunities-based care plan, the house or flat in question can be unstaffed and much more cost effective.

Here are some examples of three clients, all with severe disabilities, who might be considered for each of the three categories of accommodation. It will be noted that the disabilities, in themselves, are not the criterion for the choice of accommodation. To make this clear, we will assume that all three clients are partially sighted, have some difficulties with walking and climbing stairs and have moderate learning disabilities.

Example one – A client placed in a hostel

George, aged 42, had spent 25 years in a long-stay hospital. He had no contact with relatives. He had had little opportunity to practise daily living skills. His only friends were staff or fellow-patients, and a voluntary hospital visitor. It was expected that he would initially need a lot of support to get used to living outside hospital – although he had spent some time in a hospital training house and had had some 'training for independence' within the hospital. He would be placed with some of his friends from his ward, and a nurse from the hospital with whom he had a close relationship would continue to visit him in the hostel. After he had settled, it was anticipated that he would make new friends and also take advantage of many new opportunities which living in the community would offer. It was thus thought that while he would learn to do some things for himself – needing less support – he would need additional support to do things he had not been able to do in hospital. It could not be specified in detail in advance either what tasks he would undertake which would need support, or his pattern of living.

In this example, 'real costs' estimates would be based on the assumption that George would require a continuous staff presence during day-time, suitable cover at night-time at least initially, and access to one-to-one staff support to orientate to new surroundings and to begin to engage in new activities. It would be necessary to review 'real costs' after, say, three months, and then every six months for the first two years.

Example two – A client placed in a hostel

Mabel, aged 64, had been living with ageing parents. She had recently developed a visual impairment and had been assessed at a residential centre for people with multiple disabilities. This had given her parents respite and also made them realise they could no longer cope. Mabel herself had mixed feelings about leaving the company of her parents. A small staffed house near her parents' home would enable contact to be maintained, while Mabel would be given intensive support to learn to do some things for herself that had been done for her, and which she could do notwithstanding her disabilities.

'Real costs' in this case could be fairly accurately predicted on the basis of her support needs at the assessment centre.

Example three – A client placed in an unstaffed flat

Margaret, aged 19, had lived at home with her parents and family and had attended a special school. She was now attending a special needs course at a Further Education College. She had a close (sighted) friend and the two of them proposed to live away from their parents (although in the same locality).

In this case, the support needs (and wishes) and the 'real costs' of the proposed placement were known precisely in advance, allowing, however, for flexibility as new activities and interests developed and as greater confidence was acquired.

It may be expensive or difficult to provide 24-hour cover for unstaffed accommodation, if individual flats are widely dispersed. Hence, there are pressures to cluster unstaffed accommodation, sometimes near a staffed house. Doing this may conflict with the client's choice to live in a particular place, and it may complicate the detailed implementation of a proposed care package if other elements in the package are less accessible on this account.

A REAL COSTS ASSESSMENT

We come now to explain in more detail the actual operation of a real costs assessment.

The first point to note is that costing must be based on a thorough knowledge of what is being costed. This is the main reason why we incorporate the costing assessment in the general holistic assessment procedures. To start with costing, apart from a needs assessment, is wasteful, because we need to know about the client's needs and about the services they are receiving in order to cost them.

Within the framework of a holistic assessment, we need to know:

1. The costing implications of the client's present support needs.

2. Costing implications for additional support likely to be required in the future.

3. The costs of other existing formal services and likely adjustments to these in the future.

We will explain each of these in turn.

1. The costing implications of the client's present support needs

The costing element in care management concerns the comparison of the costs of various options. In the context of providing supported accommodation, it concerns, in particular, the comparison of the costs of the present service(s) with those envisaged as possibilities for future placements. We have suggested that present services need to be costed in terms of the client's real support needs, rather than in terms of notional needs represented by unit costs.

The questions to address are:

- What support does the client currently receive?
- What does this support cost?

We use staff diaries, kept for a fortnight, alongside client diaries, to determine the staff inputs for each client in a supported accommodation situation. We recommend that these diaries are kept initially at six-monthly intervals in order to monitor summer and winter needs.

The format for the staff diaries is shown in Figure 6 (page 54). The client diaries (see Figure 8) and the network drawings made from them (see Figures 9 and 10) provide further details and contextual information about the activities listed in the first column – which need therefore only be listed in a short form in the staff diary. For example 'breakfast' beside '8.0 am' in the staff diary tells us all we need to know in the staff diary. The Support Needs section of the Assessment Instrument (see page 45) will also tell us precisely what support or assistance was needed at breakfast.

The question for costing is to know what proportion of staff time was needed by the client at any given time of the day or night – in the case given, at breakfast. The staff diary therefore records:

- How many residents were involved in having breakfast together?
- How many staff were involved?
- How much time and attention did the client in question need in relation to the demands of the other clients at breakfast?

A simple code is suggested for answering the last question: did the client need:

- 1:1 attention (Coded A)
- Less than 1:1 but more than others in the group (Coded B)
- Average attention compared with others in the group (Coded C)
- Less than others in the group (Coded D)
- No staff time at all (Coded E)
- Other answers (to be coded according to the explanation given).

These codes are interpreted for costing purposes as follows:

Code A – 100% of staff time (one member of staff).

Code B – 150% of staff-client ratio

Code C – 100% of staff-client ratio

Code D – 50% of staff-client ratio

Code E – Zero

To take an example, suppose that: a client requires more than average staff attention at breakfast (coded B); there are two staff on duty and six clients. The staff-client ratio is 2:6 (1:3) or 0.33. The usage of staff time by this client at breakfast is estimated as being more than for average, which we cluster as 150 per cent of 0.33 = 0.5. In other words, we are assuming that the equivalent of half the time of one member of staff was devoted to the support needs of this client during breakfast.

We calculate time spent on an hourly basis. In other words, if breakfast is entered in the diary for the period 8.0 to 9.0, we assume a full hour. 'Breakfast', as we have said, is simply a label for what was going on during that hour – it might have included time spent getting the breakfast table ready, clearing the dishes afterwards or other things.

Staff support time for the client is aggregated for the fortnight and multiplied by 26 for the year (or less if the client did not attend for the full year).

During the research we then did complicated calculations for the salary costs of different members of staff. We concluded that this was unnecessary. The differential staff costs are hardly significant when it may be accidental in a supported accommodation situation which staff members are involved. For example, it might be a matter of accident whether it is, on a given occasion, the care assistant or the officer-in-charge who is helping a given client with breakfast.

This would not apply for an activity entered regularly in the diary for additional specialist input – for example physiotherapy. This would be costed separately. But for regular care and support duties we concluded it was sufficient to take the staff costs for the unit as a whole for a year, divide by the number of full-time staff (equivalent), the average number of hours worked by full-time staff in a year, and multiply by the aggregated figure of hours from the staff diaries. The 'average number of hours' worked by staff refers to the actual hours worked, including paid overtime, after deducting holidays, sick leave, and so on.

To take an example:

Staffing costs (gross) for the year:	110,000
Divide by number of FT staff* (8):	13,750*
Divide by hours worked in a year* by staff (average) – say 1680:	8.18
Multiplied by aggregated hours X 26 from staff diaries – say 900:	7,362.00

£7,362, then, is the estimated 'real cost' for staff support for this client in this residential situation.

It is possible to make the equation more sophisticated. For example, where meals are provided by cooks employed solely for cooking meals, their costs might be regarded as fixed, and therefore assessed for each resident on a unit-cost basis. The main variable costs relate to care and support staff.

The next step is to add fixed (unit) costs to the figure for variable 'real costs'. A short-cut may be simply to add a unit cost figure for the remainder of the total revenue budget.

For example:

Suppose the total revenue expenditure for the home was £170,000. Suppose there were ten residents in total. The staffing costs have already been given as £110,000, leaving £60,000 for other costs. This gives a unit figure for fixed costs of £6,000, which should be added to the 'real cost' estimate for the client we are considering (£7362) making a total estimated real cost for this client of £13,362. We then round this figure to the nearest £500 (to emphasise it can be regarded only as a guide) – i.e., £13,500.

This figure, however, may not be the true total real cost. We have found in our research (including research which entailed looking into costing procedures used by housing associations) that, unfortunately, there are no standard accounting conventions regarding

---

* It is sufficient to use the gross figure of the total number of hours worked by all staff – in this case 8 X £1,680 = £13,440 and divide the total staffing costs by this figure.

items to be included or not included in presenting figures for revenue expenditure. We suggest the following conventions:

- Items of equipment should be costed in terms of replacement for revenue purposes (i.e., their cost spread over the expected number of years of their use before they would have to be replaced). Items relating solely to one specific client are attributable to the costs of the service for that client (to add to the variable costs) but if they are items of personal equipment to cope with disabilities and the client would require these in any case wherever the placement was (e.g. a hearing aid or wheelchair) they would be excluded from the placement costs altogether.

- Interest on capital loans to be excluded.

- Administrative overheads, both on-site and off-site, to be included (Large organisations may tend to under-estimate their overheads. For our research, we used a default estimate of 40 per cent of net revenue costs as overheads).

- Voids (unfilled places) to be included in calculating unit costs (and any allowance for voids included in the income). (This can be quite complicated. Permanently unfilled vacancies for which no income is received should be disregarded).

- We suggest that staff training costs should be included in variable staff costs – as, of course, should superannuation and so forth. Recruitment and development costs should be included in overheads or otherwise counted as fixed costs. Development income should, in this case, be included on the income side.

- Where the proprietor of a venture is personally engaged in the work with clients (as distinct from administration), a figure should be given for a notional 'salary' to be included in the variable salary costs.

- In the case of a commercial venture, overheads should include a reasonable allowance for profit or return on capital.

The verification for the effectiveness of these costing procedures and conventions is that the total of the 'real costs' for all the clients in a given accommodation project should add up to the total expenditure for the project. In other words, 'real costs' are only a fairer way than unit costs of apportioning total costs.

2. Costing implications for additional support likely to be required in the future

Apart from giving information which is used for costing current services, the staff diaries show patterns of staff support for each client: for example times of the day when there are peak demands, few demands, no demands and similar possible variations for different days of the week (see Chapter Two). For both service planning and costing purposes, we need to know how this pattern is likely to change in the light of the assessment. For example, to pursue the example of time given to support a client over breakfast, supposing it is planned to give the client greater independence in preparing her own breakfast in a flat instead of with others in a communal dining room, what will be the staffing implications?

A framework for considering these issues incorporates the following concepts (see Chapter Five):

- *Growth Points.* Granted the information about current support given and current support needs, and granted client wishes (motivation) and opportunities, what should come next? What are the resource implications? For example, more or less staff time, other resources such as transport, equipment.

- *Enhancements.* A plan should never simply be to move from A to B or to stay at A. It should incorporate a second question, with what enhancements? What can improve the new placement if the client moves? What can improve the placement if the client stays? What are the resource implications? (see Chapter Five).

3. The costs of other existing formal services and likely adjustments to these in the future

When comparing present and future service costs, there are advantages in thinking in terms of global costs rather than just the costs of a principal service. The service components to be costed will include:

- supported accommodation costs (including on-site and off-site support)

- day service or other day activity costs
- specialist domiciliary services.

Services which are normally available to anyone are excluded (e.g. further education, normal health services, leisure facilities).

The main reason for preferring a global approach to service costing is that it helps us to compare costs more effectively than we would be able to do on the basis of separate agency costs alone. Different agencies cannot always be compared in terms of what they provide. For example, some supported accommodation facilities will also include day services. Some day services will include domestic training which, in other situations, will be provided in supported accommodation settings. Some facilities will have their own specialist services, and so on. These differences will not matter if we are, in any case, calculating costs in global terms.

Day service costs can be assessed using the same approach, and the staff diary form we suggested for assessing supported accommodation costs. The main variant from unit costs is likely to be in terms of the number of hours/days different clients may be attending.

Specialist services can be costed on the basis of the total costs of that service calculated at an hourly rate. For example, what does one hour of physiotherapy cost? How many hours per year does this client receive?

A problem arises in considering supported housing costs. In ordinary housing, rent and other housing services are excluded since they are available to any tenant. But where do we draw the line when housing for special needs includes services which could be regarded as care, rather than as housing functions? This issue, which has been exercising housing associations, has not been satisfactorily resolved in all cases. The issue is further confused where social service agencies incorporate accommodation costs, along with care costs, in their costing and charges without making a distinction. A rule of thumb may be to regard functions which would normally be within the limits of housing benefit as housing functions, not to be included in global costs for care management purposes.

Having arrived at a figure for global costs of all special services, the care manager is in a position to make comparisons between the costs of present services and the costs of service plans, including enhancements.

For example, let us suppose a client's present global 'real' costs are as follows:

(a) Costs of care and other services from hostel (less a
    deduction for the housing element).........................£14,000

    Day service costs £3,500

    Specialist service costs... ....£1,000

                    Total global costs £18,500

(b) Costs of proposed placement to supported flat
    (Support services only)...£8,000

    Day service costs £4,000

    Specialist service costs...£1,500

                    Total global costs £13,500

                    Net saving £5,000

A third figure is necessary in the cost comparison. This is the estimated costs in the future if the client does not move to the flat, but remains where they are in the hostel. This might not be the same as the current costs because the total number of clients in the hostel may be reducing in any case (thus increasing unit costs) or because certain enhancements would be expected in the hostel situation (e.g. increased specialist services) in the future.

4. The costs of informal support

How far should we take informal support costs into account and, if we do take them into account, how are they costed?

Our research reinforced the enhancement value of such services. Better placement outcomes were associated with larger informal service inputs.

There are, perhaps, two aspects to this issue. The first is the costs of living with informal carers at home. In this case it seems reasonable to cost the financial benefits, if any, received by the carer for caring (including tax allowances).

Second, whether the client is at home with carers or elsewhere, what about the services of volunteers? There are various ways of looking at this problem, but the procedure we favour is based on asking the question: 'If the volunteer was not providing the service, would the client be entitled to expect a similar service from a paid source?' If so, what would this service be likely to cost? If not, incidental costs claimed by the volunteer should still be recognised (e.g. travel expenses).

Guidelines in considering what a client is entitled to expect should be based on the guidelines for good practice outlined in Chapter One. For example, we would suggest that clients are entitled to annual holidays. Where these are arranged within the auspices of supported accommodation, they would obviously be included in the services costed for that facility. But where the agency providing the supported accommodation uses volunteers to provide holidays, their services should be costed as if they were care staff.

COSTS AND FEES

The main purpose and advantage of using a 'real costs' rather than a 'unit costing' approach, and in applying this approach to global rather single service costs, are to facilitate real cost comparisons. We have shown that this can help service planning and development and that, without this approach, the needs of some clients may be rejected because of apparent rather than real costs implications.

It would be logical to try to base fees actually charged for services on a real costs basis. We recommend that care managers should exercise pressures in this direction. The present reality, however, is that most agencies are accustomed to fee-charging on a unit cost basis, but sometimes with additional charges for 'extras'. The fact that there are sometimes additional charges may be a way in to change the basis of fee-charging.

For example, suppose a home for the elderly has a standard fee based on unit costs, but then charges for certain extras – chiropody, holidays, certain activities or other things. It is illogical when an able-bodied resident requiring minimum care and support is being charged as much as a resident requiring constant attention.

In this sort of situation, charging real costs may be resisted because it seems, on the face of it, 'unfair'. Why should Client A be charged more than Client B just because Client A has, perhaps, greater disabilities?

The answer to this feeling must be that costing is about realities, not equities. Far greater inequities can follow in service planning if costing is not based on realities.

CHAPTER SEVEN

Approaches to Placement Planning

Local authorities have adopted different planning approaches to care in the community and these can be broadly placed along a continuum from centralisation to a more localised approach. Our research studied the features of each type of approach.

The characteristics and issues associated with a centralised approach are:

- The main liaison with other bodies (e.g. health boards) is at a high level. Does this produce the most effective working relationships at a local level? Sometimes there is there a tendency for attitudes towards other agencies to become 'politicised'.

- There is a tendency to make large-scale deals between agencies regarding the allocation of placements. This sometimes inhibits local needs-led planning initiatives from being successful.

- Research into area or client-group needs is conducted centrally. In one case, the research findings revealed a high level of unmet need and a lack of resources to respond. This led to a local sense of frustration that 'nothing could be done'.

- Resource allocation was centralised. This led to a sense of local powerlessness over the level of resources allocated. It also led to a suspicion of any attempt to reform costing procedures in case this should lead to reduced grants being received.

- A tendency to think in terms of large projects requiring capital investment rather than small local placements needing less capital but greater revenue expenditure for support services.

- A tendency to think in terms of numbers, schemes and projects rather than in terms of individual people.
- A tendency towards a 'suitability' rather than an 'opportunities' approach to assessment (see Chapter Two).
- A working environment possibly less conducive to participation of the independent sector in service provision and in new initiatives.

Local authorities – large ones especially – have had to adapt from centralised traditions in planning and resource allocation to what we call a 'localised approach' which is more consistent with the ideals of care management. Some functions are rightly centralised – for example, the legal and financial expertise associated with purchasing and contracts can be sensibly centralised. But the key processes of resource allocation, resource targeting and placement planning should be localised.

We use the word 'localised' rather than 'decentralised' because we are not necessarily thinking in terms of administrative units. We are concerned with decision-making processes. Localisation can lead to 'street-level' influences on decision-making – especially in terms of housing allocation. By this we mean that someone who knows the street has a key role in determining which house might be allocated to a client. The advantage of this was pointed out by a respondent in our research who told us that she felt that she could have played a more useful role in a housing liaison meeting than her senior manager because she knew the area and could say immediately whether a particular property was suitable or not for a proposed placement development.

The principle of localisation is more subtle than decentralised area responsibilities. It is about involving staff from different agencies and other key people in the community (some of whom, for example, may be carers) who, because of their community involvement, can contribute to a more effective assessment and resource allocation process. Who takes the decisions may be less important for localised planning than who influences them.

The advantages of a localised approach are:

- Assessment and care management take place closer to the client and also closer to those working with the client (support staff and/or informal carers).
- Client choice has a more immediate impact on decision-making.
- The process from assessment to care packaging, resource allocation and planning is less likely to be fragmented (see Chapter Five).
- Greater flexibility.
- Better use of local resources.
- More optimistic staff attitudes.

A localised approach means that there will be flexibility in interpreting a central policy. There has to be a central policy. Indeed, with a localised approach it is all the more important that aims, principles and methods are spelt out in terms of guidelines and, where necessary, standard procedures and rules.

We will now outline in more detail what a localised approach means for each of the stages of assessment and care management.

ASSESSMENT

The notion of 'opportunities', guides the assessment method and process. Information about local opportunities will be supplemented by a knowledge of opportunities in other areas. Thus a good network of intelligence has to be in place.

We suggested in Chapter Two that data recording and data gathering should be distinguished. The principle of localisation applies to the process of involving those who are in direct daily contact with the client in data gathering and in understanding and valuing their contribution.

To value the contribution of local staff means that they should receive adequate training in assessment along the lines suggested in Chapter Four.

We have suggested (Chapter Six) that service costing should be undertaken alongside the assessment of client needs. This means that those in daily contact with the client who contribute to the assessment should be helped to understand costing issues. In turn, this will help to sustain a sense of shared localised responsibility for all aspects of the assessment task.

FROM ASSESSMENT TO SERVICE PLANNING

The principle of localisation implies client and carer involvement in a continuous process of assessing needs and preferences, considering options and making plans. It implies participation with the client in this process. In Chapter Five we stressed the importance of attention to detail in care packaging – knowing about the implications for access to local services of any care plans, for example.

This is possible if the client, and those acting with the client (informal carers, advocates or whoever else may be involved), feel a direct responsibility for this stage of care management. Assessment is something undertaken *with* the client. The implications of the assessment are shared *with* the client. Participation, as we suggested in Chapter Five, underpins every aspect of the process of care packaging.

Within this scenario, the care manager is an enabler and facilitator rather than a traditional 'manager'. He or she works with the carers and the client, bringing to the situation a wider experience of working with other carers and other clients in other localities. But he or she relies on the client to provide the information on which judgements can be made and shared.

Assessments and service plans that we have undertaken, using the assessment instrument presented in Chapter Two, include these features:

- Following an initial interview with the client and immediate carers (at home or in supported accommodation), the first parts of the assessment are completed. Diaries are left with the client.

- A draft of the care manager's initial reflections on the assessment is shared with the client/carers.

- Further information is gathered when the diaries are collected. The first reflections are discussed.

- Other agencies with input to the assessment are contacted.

- A draft of a completed assessment, and service plans, are shared with the client/carer.

By these means there is a continuous process from assessment to care planning involving the client and informal carers.

FROM SERVICE PLANNING TO RESOURCE ALLOCATION

There has been much debate, as well as varied practices, within care management about devolved budgets. Much depends on the form devolved budgets will take and how they are conceived. What we are concerned with, from the point of view of localisation, is not so much the question of who holds the budget, but of access to it and how responsive holders (whoever they are) are to local interests, local responsibilities and local initiatives.

For example, one local authority studied in our research had a small top-up budget called an independent living fund. This was accessible to local care managers to finance enhancements to placements to be used at their discretion. The fact that the budget was held centrally did not in this case reduce its usefulness for local initiatives, in the context of a localised approach to assessment and care management.

Devolved budgets are justified if they favour an individualised, flexible approach to resource allocation.

The research found varied attitudes towards resource allocation which we called 'passive' and 'active'. A passive attitude, which tended to dominate where there was a more centralised approach to care management, was characterised by waiting passively for somebody else to allocate resources so that, when the resources arrived, care plans could be implemented. An 'active' attitude, on the other hand, was characterised by local managers feeling they had some control over resources which they could actively seek to maximise beyond what central funding mechanisms might supply. They might, for example, be more actively involved with the client in applying for additional funds from independent sources, or, for larger enterprises, from outside funding sources.

A localised approach needs to be supported by centrally-provided expertise in procuring external funds. We are not suggesting that care managers turn professional fund-raisers, but that they should be actively aware of resource opportunities. Some local authorities employ community workers (or staff with other titles performing this role) in the community care field who can support local client or carers' groups in obtaining funds and other resources. Whoever does this task, local authorities need to exercise an enabling role so that individuals and groups in the community can play an effective part in service provision and resource procurement. It should not just be a case of 'leaving it to the independent sector'.

Thus, although care in the community favours a purchaser/provider split, there is no suggestion that the two should not be working together to maximise resources. The care manager, as purchaser, should be able to make suggestions to a service provider as to how funding (or other resources) could be increased and obtained from a variety of sources to enhance the benefits to the client.

Often service providers in the independent sector are alive to funding possibilities from different sources. Where services are still run by local authorities themselves, they may not be as alive to such possibilities in all areas. But even in the independent sector, our research has suggested that there can be very varied rates of take-up of available grants.

A localised approach means thinking in terms of individual clients instead of in terms of projects and schemes for dealing with numbers. This runs counter to traditional practice. For example, an agency can hardly make use of such funding mechanisms as the EEC or large private trusts on the basis of the needs of an individual client in isolation. There are pressures to think in terms of schemes or projects rather than people. These pressures, in turn, may lead to unnecessarily elaborate schemes – for example purpose-designed buildings where mainstream housing would suffice.

Sometimes new projects involving service planning for a group of clients will be required. The question arises as to how planning can be 'needs-led' when resource procurement and planning are often a slow and uncertain business. For example, in one case, where a needs-led approach was strictly adhered to, the building was only erected four years after the needs of the individual clients had been identified. Thus, it is more common to obtain the resources for a project and to begin work on the basis of what may be called 'planning assessments', than on detailed assessments of the needs of individual clients. The detailed service planning then influences adjustments and adaptations to the buildings. Here are some examples of situations with which we have been associated where service plans (initiated by carers) have been supported:

1. Example one

A group of parents joined a voluntary agency and raised the money for a detailed needs assessment of adults with severe or profound learning disabilities in their locality. Proposals which ensued included a house for five people. The agency purchased a suitable house and necessary adaptations were made using local authority funding supplemented by funds raised voluntarily. There was an interval of about 18 months between the individual assessments and the opening of the house – by which time one potential client had withdrawn and a substitute was someone who had not been included in the original assessment.

2. Example two

A group of parents of children and adults with profound learning disabilities successfully applied for Urban Aid funding for a special day service. To avoid raising expectations which could not be fulfilled, the assessment of potential users was delayed until resources had been assured and the plans agreed. This meant that the plans for the building and the level of staffing could not be radically altered at the time the needs were assessed. Staffing deployment (i.e., what kinds of staff should be appointed) and furnishing and equipment could be influenced, however, by the assessment. More important, perhaps, the assessment, based on a survey of the needs of everyone in the locality who might have a profound learning disability, gave a profile of needs in terms of numbers and range, and this influenced decisions about priorities in admissions, and whether attendance should be part-time or full-time.

In both these examples, the planning assessments and the individual client-needs assessments were combined. That it to say, there was a survey of needs for the particular client group in given localities together with a holistic assessment, based on an opportunities approach, of each client. These assessments were followed through in terms of individual and group service plans and resource implications. The difference was that in Example (1), the resources were procured after the assessment had been undertaken; in example (2) the resources were procured in advance.

Which procedure is followed must vary in individual circumstances but on the following conditions:

1. If *the assessments take place first* there must a reasonable expectation that resources will follow, otherwise hopes will have been unfairly raised. Plans must be made beforehand to facilitate quick implementation once the assessments are completed and the resource allocation confirmed.

2. *If resources are found first* plans must be flexible enough to allow for a needs-led implementation.

In the case of a centralised rather than a localised approach, the procedure would be more likely to involve a two-stage assessment as follows:

> *Stage One* A planning assessment. This means a survey of the numbers and range of needs of a particular client group in a given geographical area. Methods for undertaking this, for example in the field of dementia, are currently being developed in Tayside Region in Scotland. Following Bond and Carstairs (1982), 'dimensions of need' were recorded for all clients referred from the widest range of sources (Gordon 1992, Spicker *et al.* 1993). It may be noted that this research provides a basis for planning which is much more sophisticated and reliable than using general studies of prevalence rates, although prevalence rates do provide useful reference material. Nonetheless three points should be noted:
>
> - Planning assessments only provide a minimum of information about clients. They do not take the place of individual assessments, which are required for care in the community.
>
> - Planning assessments provide a profile of needs – they do not purport to tell planners how they should respond to needs. For example, a planning assessment can provide information about various dimensions to support needs, details about the characteristics of the client population and current sources of support. It cannot tell the planners whether they should respond in terms of more residential provision or in terms of more intensive domiciliary support. This, it is claimed, is a policy role.

- Planning assessments of the kind described do not tell us anything about client views.

From the perspective of a localised approach to service planning, such planning assessments are of value in providing a basis for quantifying estimates of resources to be required over a wide area and districts within the area. They do not inform detailed local planning or resource targeting in response to needs, if such a response is to be truly on a client-needs basis, as illustrated in the two examples quoted earlier.

RESOURCE ALLOCATION AND RESOURCE TARGETING

'Allocation' refers to the resources available or received from particular sources – for example, a budget allocation means a given amount of money for a particular purpose in a particular area and often for a particular client group. 'Targeting' refers to the distribution made of the resources that have been allocated to meet the needs of particular clients or groups of clients.

To go back to the example we used in Chapter Six when we were considering approaches to costing:

> It was planned to disperse the residents of a hostel to smaller units in the community. Those residents with least support needs were to be accommodated in flats with off-site support. Those with greater support needs were to be accommodated in smaller staffed houses. A sum of money had been estimated, prior to the individual assessments, for the project. This sum constituted the resources that had been allocated. However, it was insufficient to meet both categories of need – for both staffed and unstaffed flats. A decision was taken to give priority to the clients requiring unstaffed accommodation.

This can be referred to as resource 'targeting'.

With a centralised approach to service planning, and a passive attitude to resource procurement, the distinction between resource allocation and targeting is important. Resource allocation represents the 'cake'; targeting refers to how the 'cake' is divided. However, with a localised approach to service planning and a more active attitude to resource procurement, the processes of allocation and targeting become aligned. There is also, perhaps, a broader perception of resources than that simply of money.

For example, an alternative approach to the dispersal of residents from the hostel described above would have been to analyse existing informal sources of support in the locality for the clients and then consider what support was needed to enable the clients to live as lodgers (instead of in staffed accommodation) or with neighbour support (instead of unstaffed supported accommodation). Resources are only allocated when the 'targets' in terms of people offering support have been identified.

Whatever approach is adopted, there will be situations when resources are not available. Within a centralised approach, the lack of resources can lead to a sense of gloom amongst staff, who feel there is nothing they can do. Within a localised approach, staff are in a better position to understand the resource problems. They are also often in a position to demonstrate that the inability to provide resources to provide highly cost-effective support, as in the example above, would result in greater expenditure in the longer run. The consequence of failing to find the resources to support an informal carer may mean that a client has to be accommodated in some form of staffed accommodation at much greater cost.

MONITORING AND EVALUATION

Monitoring means systematically examining what has happened or what is happening in practice. Evaluation means reviewing services and their outcomes. The methods are similar. If monitoring takes place regularly, an evaluation will be based on drawing together information obtained from monitoring.

Monitoring should be undertaken in respect of (i) placement decisions and their implementation and (ii) standards of practice within placements.

For monitoring placements, we recommend a procedure adapted from our research. The format for a form for monitoring individual placement outcomes is shown in Figure 18. The form is, ideally, completed by a care manager, or staff member acting on his behalf, and the client. Any disagreements between those completing the form are recorded at the end.

The first part of the placement monitoring form establishes what the outcome was and the second part asks for views, first in general terms and, second, in terms of factors influencing the decision. Respondents are asked to give ratings for possible factors which affected the outcome. In particular, it will register the extent to which client's choice, placement availability and resource allocation influenced the outcome. This procedure may be used as a way of monitoring care management.

Standards of practice in providing services, once the placement has taken place, are monitored using parts of the assessment Instrument described in Chapter Two. A 'value for money' aspect of this is the minimal use of care management time. The essential evidence on which a service will be monitored is obtained from client and staff diaries.

A summary form for a short review of progress and other changes that have taken place since a previous evaluation is shown in Figures 19 and 20. Figure 19 is the front 'cover' and Figure 20 provides updates for subsequent pages. A network diagram based on the diaries would also be included with these summaries.

These forms may be regarded as standard, whether the agency follows a centralised or a localised approach to care management. The approach will, however, affect the process of information-gathering. A localised approach is likely to favour participation with the client in the monitoring process.

Information about me . . . . (Name)
to help to plan for the future.

When completed . . . . (Date)

This part is completed by . . . . (. . . . .)*

         with help from . . . . (. . . . .)*

* State position e.g. resident, key worker, care manager

---

1. What option was chosen (in the plan as implemented)

(i) To stay where I am: YES/NO
    If *yes*, with what additional services or other enhancements? . . . .
    . . . .
    1.
    2.
    3.

Figure 18 Monitoring of placement outcomes

(ii) To move to a new placement: YES/NO
     If *yes*, where to? . . . .
     With what additional services or other enhancements?
     1.
     2.
     3.

2. Do . . . . regard the option as: (*tick below and comment*)
     Ideal.
     Less than ideal but still a good decision.
     Not ideal and in many ways unfortunate.
     Temporary – simply a waiting decision while other
          possibilities are awaited.
     Other answers.

3. Rank the following factors in order of maximum influence
   on the placement outcome: (*place a number '1' beside the
   most important factor, '2' beside the next most important, and
   so on. Place a '0' if the factor was of no importance at all*)

   Client's choice   ☐
   Relative's wishes   ☐
   Competing demands for limited places   ☐
   Cheapness of the option and expense of
        other possibilities   ☐
   Availability of housing or other buildings   ☐
   Influence of agency policies   ☐
   Other factors (state)   ☐
   Comment: ☐

4. Were you (the client) personally involved in the decision
   AFTER the assessment had been completed? . . . .
   . . . .

5. Add any other comments from the client: . . . .
   . . . .

6. Were there any disagreements between the client and the
   care manager in completing this form? If so, explain: . . .
   . . . .

Figure 18 Monitoring of placement outcomes (continued)

Name   Reference
Care Manager   Key Worker   Date:
(1st change):   Date:
(2nd change):   Date:

D.O.B.   Gender: Next of Kin:
Where living at present: Date:
(1st change):   Date:
(2nd change):   Date:

Social background: . . . .
. . . .
. . . .
Previous accomodation history (brief details): . . . .
. . . .
. . . .
Schooling: . . . .
. . . .
. . . .
After leaving school
(main employment/day service/FE etc.): . . . .
. . . .
. . . .
Others in household and their relationship to client:
Name: *Relationship to client:*
. . . .
. . . .
. . . .
(Delete and add to update).

Figure 19 'Front cover' for short review of progress

Support needs (summary statements) page:

Assessment/review Date:	
Self management growth points	Recent progress or regress
Daily living growth points	
Interests and support needed	
Health problems and disabilities	Recent improvement or deterioration

Assessment/review Date:	
Self management growth points	Recent progress or regress
Daily living growth points	
Interests and support needed	
Health problems and disabilities	Recent improvement or deterioration

Figure 20 Updates page for short review of progress

CONFIDENTIALITY AND SECURITY

The approach adopted will also affect attitudes towards confidentiality and security. Information stored on computer (as this is likely to be) must conform to the data protection legislation. We recommend inverting the traditional approach to a hierarchy of security for access to data stored on a computer. Computer software usually assumes that 'top management' has unlimited access, while subordinates have limited access to data. We propose, instead, that the fine detail of assessment and care management need only be accessible to care managers and key workers while the general information relevant to planning is the legitimate concern of higher management. There are, nonetheless, exceptional circumstances in which the highest management will need to know the minutest details – for example when facing serious allegations of abuse.

CHAPTER 8

People with Very Special Needs

People with 'very special needs' are those whose needs are complex and who require highly individualised assessment and care management, drawing on a specialist knowledge.

Sometimes there is a tendency to see people's support needs in simplified quantitative rather than qualitative terms. We talk about 'high' and 'low' levels of dependency or of 'maximum' and 'minimum' risks. We tend to think of an assessment in terms of 'how much' support a client needs.

People whom we have defined as having 'very special needs' help us to question this traditional over-simplification. In quantitative terms, it is true, most (but not all) people with very special needs are at the 'high' end of the continuum. But if we take a very small group, for example those who have multiple disabilities including profound intellectual impairment, we find extreme heterogeneity or variety of different kinds of support needs. Similarly, if we take a group such as those suffering from a life-threatening illness, we find qualitative differences and differing support implications in qualitative as well as in quantitative terms. The same is true for a third group, namely people with so-called 'challenging behaviour'. It would apply no less to a fourth main group: those with problems related to serious addictions.

It follows that the assessment and care management of people with very special needs requires a sensitivity to individual differences and a knowledge of specific syndromes or illnesses that may help to account for some (not all) aspects of these differences. We stress *not all* because whatever a person's health or medical condition, individual personality plays a key part in their lives and in assessing their needs.

With these general points in mind, let us look at some specific assessment and care management issues for the four main groups we have referred to, namely:

1. People with multiple disabilities.

2. People with a life-threatening illness.

3. People with challenging behaviour.

4. People with problems related to serious addictions.

Each of these groups include many sub-groups, as well as a plethora of labels.

1. People with multiple disabilities

More people with a disability than many of us recognise will have *multiple* disabilities. For example, many people whom we categorise as having 'learning disabilities' will also have other physical disabilities or sensory impairments. Because they are labelled as having a learning disabilility or a mental handicap, their other problems may be underrated or ignored.

The assessment should therefore be sensitive to the many dimensions to multiple disability:

- different kinds and aspects of physical and mental disability

- sensory impairments including visual and hearing impairment especially

- epilepsy (which itself takes very different forms with different implications for daily living and support needs).

We single out epilepsy because it is common and because it involves particular complications. In our view it receives insufficient attention, tending to fall between different medical specialisms – psychiatry, neurology, pharmacology. The care manager should know where to turn for all-round expert advice, perhaps through one of the epilepsy associations, the largest being the British Epilepsy Association.*

---

* The British Epilepsy Association. Anstey House, 40 Hanover Square, Leeds LS3 1BE. For Scotland there is also The Epilepsy Association of Scotland, 40 Govan Road, Glasgow G51 1Jl

We recommend that every care manager should subscribe to the *Directory of Specific Conditions and Rare Syndromes* in which basic information and contact addresses will be found on both rare and not so rare conditions.

In recent years, societies representing the visually impaired, hearing impaired and both (the 'deaf blind') have rightly been concerned that single labels for general or specific conditions may hide the sensory aspects of a person's disability. It is thus very important to ask in every assessment about possible sensory impairments and whether there has been a recent specialist examination or assessment in relation to sensory impairments.

In many instances it will be found that the potential of people with multiple disabilities has been neglected. The range of quality in schooling and in adult services is enormous. Sometimes a person with a multiple disability – for example someone with cerebral palsy – will have had a first-class schooling. In this case the question is about the let-down they and their carers have experienced when schooling ceased. Very few day services will have maintained the expectations and the development of potential that featured at school. Others will have had a poor schooling experience, while older people with multiple disabilities may sometimes have had no schooling at all. In these instances, carers' expectations of adult services may be low. The care manager has a responsibility to revive whatever hope there may have been earlier and to seek services which will provide a wide range of stimulation and challenge.

Most people with a profound or very severe mental handicap (learning disability) will have multiple disabilities. There are exceptions, and these form a small group of people whose needs are no less great but different in kind. They may be physically strong and fit but needing very substantial assistance with self-care and major support in developing opportunities for a better quality of life in daily living. They are also likely to have had a poor schooling experience – although, again, there will be major variations in the quality of schooling. Most adult day services, if they manage this client group at all, do so poorly in terms of offering the kinds of stimulation and intensive training they need. If there is a priority, it is likely to be in terms of trying to develop communication, by whatever means may be possible (and recent technology has come up with some new ideas). The sense of frustration of a fully-developed young adult, for example, who cannot make their wishes and needs known, can be imagined if we stop and think about it. Their communication often has to be through their actions, and their actions may appear to staff as idiosyncratic, challenging, and uncontrolled. The problems are confounded when, because of their strength, two rather than a single staff person may sometimes be needed – for example to escort the client in a busy street.

A major need for most people with multiple disabilities and complex special needs is space. It is vital for the care manager to know such practical details as just how much space is needed for particular individuals with particular needs, especially for people who depend on wheelchairs. The minimum size required for the bathroom/toilet is a basic consideration, and regulations on this matter are only a guide. We were involved in the assessment of needs for one very tall young man with a profound learning disability and cerebral palsy. He needed extra space to be laid out on a table in the toilet for his nappy to be changed, as well as an extra large wheelchair and an extra-sized lift to cope with it. This is an extreme example, but it does illustrate that individual needs have to be known about in detail before briefs are given to architects for buildings or adaptations for this client-group.

Another issue, particularly for people with multiple disabilities, is whether those with different kinds of needs can be supported together. Experience suggests that to arrange for people with a particular combination of disabilities to live with other people with precisely similar disabilities is socially restrictive. However, if a single person who is, for example, fairly able bodied, lives with others all of whom are frail and in wheelchairs, the care implications have to be thought about. We were recently assessing a case like this where the able-bodied client appeared not to be getting enough to eat because the menus were geared to the appetites of those leading less energetic lives!

Different issues arise in considering day services. Day services are, or should be, concerned with training – although the training will take different forms and it is for different purposes (Seed 1988) An important aim of day services is usually considered to be to promote integration with the ordinary community and to provide opportunities for people with special needs to learn skills which will facilitate greater independence for them to live in the community. It does not follow that these aims will be furthered by 'mixing' people with very different interests and needs in one programme or project. 'Integration' between people with profound and multiple disabilities and those with 'mild' disabilities has nothing to do with integration in the 'ordinary' community. Although yet to be evaluated, there are arguments in favour of small specialist day services for people with the most profound and multiple disabilities with a high multi-disciplinary service input offering intensive training, stimulation and opportunity, at the same time as care and safety are assured.

Probably a majority of people in this group has always lived at home with parents or other informal carers, but the proportion is higher today than in the past. As people with some disabilities are living longer, and as more are discharged from hospital, the pressure to provide appropriate accommodation, as well as day services, is building up. Yet we have seen in Chapter Six that this is the very group whose need for small staffed units often appears prohibitively expensive – to some extent unjustly so when compared on a false unit cost basis within large hostel accommodation. On a 'real cost' basis the difference between traditional hostel and smaller house accommodation is less great, with the latter offering usually far greater opportunities.

We suggest that care managers recognise that for a small number of people (and we are talking about very small numbers, perhaps 20–30 per 100,000 of the general population) small staffed units need to be provided for people with profound intellectual and multiple disabilities. It is right, as well as in the long run inevitable, that they should leave the care of their parents or other relatives fairly early in adulthood, thereby exercising the same right to 'independence' in that sense that others enjoy. An increasing number of parents recognise that it is right for their sons or daughters in this group to leave home while they are young rather than wait until the parents can no longer cope because of their own old age, and live preferably in local accommodation where family links can be easily maintained and where the responsibilities of care can still, to some extent, be shared.

In the meantime, parents caring at home for sons or daughters in this group do need respite, which often seems to stop when they leave school. Whatever the philosophy of day services, the reality that they also serve to provide day-time respite to carers of this group should not be minimised.

So far we have mainly discussed the needs of people whose multiple disabilities include an intellectual impairment. The term 'multiple disability' is sometimes used with this assumption, to the detriment of people with a combination of physical disabilities and sensory impairments, but with no mental impairment, whose needs appear often to be neglected. Many such people are also elderly and receive services as elderly people. It is the younger school-leaver in this group who sometimes may fall between traditional service categories when it comes to thinking about placements away from home (Seed 1992a). It is for just such people that a client-needs-led, rather than a service-led, approach to care in the community is put to the test and where effective care management to provide an appropriate service response can be vindicated. As with all people with multiple disabilities, a consideration of communication difficulties and potential should be given top priority. The second top priority will be to develop and maintain physical mobility.

2. People with a life-threatening illness

Care in the community will be concerned with four main subgroups:

- degenerative conditions specifically affecting people who are elderly, notably dementia
- life-threatening (or potentially life-threatening) illnesses affecting people of any age – for example cancer and leukemia
- inherited disorders with a degenerative prognosis – for example Rett Syndrome
- HIV infection with the threat of 'full blown' AIDs.

A theme common to all of these people is the need to recognise in assessment and care management that they have quality of life potential, that they are entitled to be regarded as people with a future, however limited or prolonged that future may turn out to be (and it can seldom be accurately predicted). Their condition does not affect the whole of their being – they are still individuals with potential in areas of life which their condition does not directly affect, of even where it does affect, and even in affected areas, progress is not totally precluded.

A second theme is to do with the natural process of grief and mourning with the initial disclosure of their conditions and of its implications – both for themselves and for those who are nearest and dearest to them.

A third theme concerns the importance of a holistic approach, recognising the significance of a healthy environment, as well as of the part played in their lives by friends and sometimes relatives. The kind of holistic approach to assessment we have suggested in Chapter Two for all clients is especially useful for people in these groups.

A fourth theme, which follows from the first three, is to be ready to transfer social work care and support skills and methods from work with other client groups and adapt and apply them to these groups of people. This has been spelt out, for example, in the Case Studies for Practice series dealing with dementia (Chapman and Marshall 1993), and HIV and AIDS (Gaitley and Seed 1989). Because social workers, like others, may sometimes be prone to an initial fear of life-threatening illnesses, they may hive the work off to a few specialists without recognising what their own generic social work skills have to offer. Of course, there are special aspects of each condition, where the specific implications need to be appreciated. In the case of inherited disorders, as well as for other potentially life-threatening conditions such as cancer, we would again refer the reader wanting specialist information and contacts to the *Directory of Specific Conditions and Rare Syndromes*.

3. People with challenging behaviour

This is a currently fashionable term applied particularly to people with learning disabilities who present behaviour problems, especially in care settings. Perhaps no less challenging for responsible care management is the behaviour of:

- some people with mental health problems
- some young people leaving care or special schools who are 'emotionally damaged'
- some ex-prisoners, including some sex-offenders
- some people who themselves have been sexually abused
- some people who have suffered severe head injuries
- some people suffering from dementia.

It will be noted that we have begun each sub-group within a broader than customary interpretation of 'challenging behaviour' with the word 'some'. *Some* people with mental health problems, *some* ex-prisoners, and so on, but not *all* such people present very special needs on account of their behaviour. Others in each of these groups do not present such problems and care managers, like the general public, must avoid stereotyping assumed behaviour patterns associated with particular labels or sets of circumstances.

Sometimes the label 'challenging behaviour' may be inappropriately applied – when the behaviour that care staff find 'challenging' reflects the restrictions of the care regime in being able to meet the client's needs. The following is an example from our research:

Jim

> Jim, who could only speak a few words, could participate in little of the normal social interchange in the hospital ward of 30 patients, where he shared a 'bedroom' with five others. His diary showed that he spent most of his day 'dotting to and fro' between the ward and the main hall of the hospital, where the social therapy unit ran a social club. The constant coming and going was apparently a problem for ward staff, who tried to make him stay in one place.

> The diary recorded that one morning when Jim returned to the ward for the umpteenth time, the staff became exasperated when he refused to go back to the hall. Staff said he became 'disruptive'. He was given a sedative. During the remainder of the day he was recorded as having slept in a chair most of the time.

> The assessment asked what Jim liked to do 'at home' (in his case, 'home' being hospital). Since he could not speak sufficiently, staff answered the question on his behalf: 'sitting watching what other people are doing; attracting staff and residents' attention by banging my chair on the ground; repeatedly moving around from chair to chair in the day room'.

Most of the above behaviour might seem objectively understandable, but in the context of the ward it was regarded as presenting a 'challenge' because of the social crowding of his environment.

Many examples could be quoted from our experience of such clients quickly changing their patterns of behaviour in more congenial surroundings, and with more personal attention, in smaller units in the community.

There are two sets of problems with 'challenging behaviour'. First, people can be trapped into staying in uncongenial surroundings just because of their behaviour. They must change their behaviour before they are considered 'ready' to move, but they cannot do so *until* they move. This issue may be addressed by getting away from a 'readiness' approach to assessment and by being prepared to take risks, with appropriate support, to provide new opportunities in the care plan.

Second, however, some people will present behavioural issues wherever they live. In this case, changing the placement environment is not going to help and may only cause confusion. Especially if the placement has long-term advantages, or meets basic needs in a way no other placement is likely to achieve, the behavioural issues should be addressed where they occur. This is achieved by providing the additional staffing or equipment to tackle the problems and using the kinds of skills social workers and others possess from many different fields based on an understanding of social behaviour in the context of meeting basic needs.

We mention 'equipment' because this can sometimes help. In one case, a particular kind of chair was supplied which was carefully chosen to provide a tight-fitting sense of security.

All of these suggestions are likely to be expensive – but so is *any* method of dealing with challenging behaviour in ways which protect the client and others. A custodial approach is expensive too, especially in the long run if it tries only to ameliorate rather than to remedy the situation.

Sometimes the term 'challenging behaviour' is recognised in relation to people staying in residential institutions more readily than in the case of people living in the community supported by informal carers. Care management should give no less attention to the latter than to the former. Respite, support and regular reviews of the strains and stresses as well as of opportunities are necessary. Perhaps especially important is a clear line of response to the carers in cases of emergency, thereby giving them the security they need. Challenging behaviour can take many different forms – tantrums, wandering, delinquent acts, or just constant demands – and an 'emergency' is a situation where, for whatever reason, the carers just cannot cope, granted their human limitations and the limitations of the setting. Crisis team visits may be a successful form of response in such cases.

4. People with problems related to serious addictions

Challenging behaviour may also be presented by people with serious addictions, but in this case there is an added dimension to the problem. Whether their behaviour causes problems to others or not, serious addictions eventually cause problems, often life-threatening problems, to the addict, and on this account they may be included amongst people with very special needs.

Most of us have some addictions, but they are relatively harmless – for example, many people are addicted to coffee or tea. Life-threatening or other serious addictions (e.g. drugs or drink) may be termed a 'behavioural disease' often affecting the deepest parts of a person's being. As a disease, it can affect members in every strata of society. As 'behaviour' it requires effort on the part of the sufferer to overcome it, but effort alone will not suffice. As a 'disease', an addiction needs 'treatment' – which can take many forms.

People with serious addictions will often be in the trap we described earlier, namely they cannot move to a better environment until they 'change' and they cannot change in their present environment. The addiction will be a complicating factor. The following is an example from our research of a young man with Down's Syndrome who had a drink problem:

Harry

> Harry lives in a hostel and is capable of going out and about by himself as long as main roads are not required to be crossed. The care manager completing the assessment discovered a concern amongst workers, both at the hostel and at the day centre he attended, about his drinking. Harry saw drinking as normal. It was something he saw his father do – something most people do.

> However, because of his learning disability, drinking at pubs was different for Harry. People kept buying him drinks, perhaps out of sympathy. He had been banned from some of the local pubs because he would take other people's drinks when they were not looking or when they were at the toilet.

> It was revealed that Harry had spent nights at the local hospital because he had been too drunk to find his way home. A holiday had ended abruptly because, after getting drunk, he had been sick and burst a blood vessel in his eye.

A succession of counsellors tried to help Harry – key worker in the hostel, community nurse, psychiatrist – but failed. As drinking became more of an issue, Harry became more furtive about it – nipping off to a pub from the day centre, for example, when staff were otherwise engaged and did not notice his absence.

It had been hoped that Harry would move from the hostel to more independent living in supported accommodation run by a housing association. It was considered he had the necessary ability. However, the housing association would not accept someone with behaviour problems such as those Harry presented on account of his drinking. Thus Harry remained in the hostel, due to the intractability of his problem and the lack of facilities (known to his carers) to cope with him as he is.

The following points should be noted as likely to feature with people suffering from life-threatening or other serious addictions:

- At certain stages they try to hide their habit from those caring for them.
- Those caring for them may not recognise for a time the extent of their problem.
- Satisfying their addictive habit will bring other problems to themselves and others caring for them.
- Eventually, when they reach their 'bottom line', being ill and in great discomfort, they may seek help; some will have to get to this point many times before they can really seek and accept help.
- When they are ready to be helped, the first stage is to end their dependence on their habit. The following stages constitute the reconstruction of their lives without their habit. This, in turn, means understanding the part their habit played in their life, and, if possible, why?
- People with addictions are often helped by others who have suffered from the same addiction and who have successfully 'mastered' it. (Many people with very serious addictions would never claim to have overcome them – they claim they can only live a day at

a time). Some people who have mastered their addictions find it helpful to them to try to help others. Thus group therapy (of various kinds) often features in care plans.

- Families and carers of people with addictions are profoundly affected. Other family members may benefit from contacts with others in similar situations.

Having made these points which are common to most addictions, it must be recognised that different addictions bring additional specific problems and raise other issues. A further complicating factor is the varying attitudes of society towards different addictions – tobacco, drinking, hard and soft drugs, gambling and so on.

Available services to help people with addictions vary greatly in different localities. Those areas with services often appear to attract people from other areas, and good services are suspected by the public of bringing problems in their wake.

In some cases, service provision is complicated by differing philosophical approaches – although perhaps less so today than in the past. This has especially applied to coping with drink problems, with differences about total abstinence or 'controlled drinking' and about other treatments.

Sometimes the isolation of specialist services for people with addictions has hindered a more holistic understanding of their causes and consequences. We are now beginning to be more aware of connections between addictions and child care problems, for example.

OTHERS WITH VERY SPECIAL NEEDS

The four groups of people with very special needs we have briefly discussed include most people generally thought to come into this category. But there are others: for example some people who have been homeless, including refugees; some people who have been the victims of violence; people who are the survivors of disasters or close relatives of victims (Tumelty 1990).

People who have suffered head injuries form another important group. Many have been injured as a result of road accidents when they were young, and have residual support needs which may continue into later life. Such people tend to fall between the conventional categorisation of client groups and may not, so far, have been accorded sufficient consideration in formulating priorities for care management and appropriate service provision.

The vindication of a needs-led approach to assessing and managing care in the community will be demonstrated if hitherto neglected needs are exposed and responded to with specialist knowledge, imagination and professional skill.

Further Help

We hope this book has been helpful as a short introduction to a way of approaching care in the community responsibilities.

We are available to undertake work, either doing the assessments for you or by advising you on how to do it.

This may include, for example:

- assessments of groups of clients for new service initiatives on a client-needs-led principle

- consultations with regard to the adaptation and use of the assessment instrument for both care managers and service providers

- staff training for using this approach for assessment and care-management

- evaluation of existing needs-led services, especially for projects recently established. It should be noted that an evaluation of a new service needs to begin when the service begins operating, in order to establish a base-line assessment and to monitor progress from this point.

Enquiries in the first instance should be addressed to:

Philip Seed, Tom-Na-Monachan, Cuilc Brae, Pitlochry, Perthshire, Scotland PH16 5QP. Tel: 0796 473744.

References

Bond, J. and Carstairs, V. (1982) *Services for the Elderly*. Edinburgh: SHHD.

Chapman, J. and Marshall, M. (eds) (1993) *Dementia: New Skills for Social Workers*. London: Jessica Kingsley Publishers.

Gaitley, R. and Seed, P. (1989) *HIV and AIDS – A Social Network Approach*. London: Jessica Kingsley Publishers.

Goldstein, H. (1971) *Social Work Practice – A Unitary Approach*. Columbia, SC: University of South Carolina Press.

Gordon, D.S. (1992) *Dementia Needs Assessment Project. Working Paper 5*. University of Dundee, Department of Medicine.

Hogg, J. and Raynes, N.V. (eds) (1987) *Assessment in Mental Handicap. A Guide to Assessments Practices, Tests and Checklists*. London: Croom Helm.

Hubbard, M. (1992) School Leavers with Multiple Disabilities: An Exploratory Study of the Issues and Problems Relating to Planning and Provision of Formal Post-School Services. Unpublished PhD Thesis, University of Stirling.

Rasmussen, B. and Hersom. (1987) *Habilitation Documentation. Habilitation Software*. 204, North Sterling Street, Morganton. NC 28655. USA).

Rowley, D. *et al.* (1993) *Planning and Managing Community Care*. CC3. Dundee: University of Dundee Department of Social Work.

Schalock, R.L. *et al.* (1989) Quality of life – its measurement and use. In *Mental Retardation*. Vol 27. No 1.

Seed, P. (1988) *Day Care and the Cross-Roads*. Tunbridge Wells: Costello.

Seed, P. (1990) *Introducing Network Analysis in Social Work*. London: Jessica Kingsley Publishers.

Seed, P. (1992a) *Developing Holistic Education*. Basingstoke: Falmer Press.

Seed, P. (1992b) *Assessment, Resource Allocation and Planning for Adults with Learning Disabilities. A Literature Review*. Dundee: University of Dundee, Social Work Department Publications.

Seed, P. (1993) *Assessment, Resource Allocation and Planning for Adults with Learning Disabilities in Supported Accommodation in Scotland*. A short report of research undertaken by Dundee University, Department of Social Work for Social Work Services Group of the Scottish Office 1990–92. Crown copyright.

Spicker, P. et al. (1993) *Progress Report to Funding Body*. University of Dundee, Department of Medicine.

The Directory of Specific Conditions and Rare Syndromes. Published by Contact-A-Family, 16 Strutton Ground, London SW1P 2HP.

Tumelty, D. (1990) *Social Work in the Wake of Disaster*. London: Jessica Kingsley Publishers.

University of Dundee, Social Work Department (1993) *Planning and Managing Community Care*. Dundee: University of Dundee, Social Work Department Publications.

Index